D1223894

AIR AND WATER

CHEMISTRY

Grolier Educational
SHERMAN TURNPIKE, DANBURY, CONNECTICUT 06816

First published in the United States in 1998
by Grolier Educational, Sherman Turnpike,
Danbury, CT 06816

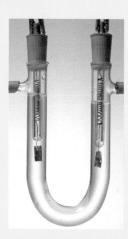

Author
Brian Knapp, BSc, PhD
Project consultant
*Keith B. Walshaw, MA, BSc, DPhil
(Head of Chemistry, Leighton Park School)*
Project Director
Duncan McCrae, BSc
Editor
Mary Sanders, BSc
Special photography
Ian Gledhill
Illustrations
The Ascenders Partnership, David Woodroffe
Electronic page makeup
The Ascenders Partnership
Designed and produced by
EARTHSCAPE EDITIONS
Print consultants
Chromo Litho Ltd
Reproduced in Malaysia by
Global Colour
Printed and bound in Italy by
L.E.G.O. SpA

Library of Congress Cataloging-in-Publication Data
ChemLab
  p. cm.
  Includes indexes.
  Contents: v.1.Gases, liquids, and solids –
v.2.Elements, compounds, and mixtures – v.3.The
periodic table – v.4.Metals – v.5.Acids, bases, and salts
– v.6.Heat and combustion – v.7.Oxidation and
reduction – v.8.Air and water chemistry – v.9.Carbon
chemistry – v.10.Energy and chemical change –
v.11.Preparations – v.12. Tests.
  ISBN 0–7172–9146–4 (set). – ISBN 0–7172–9154–5 (v.8).
  1. Chemistry – Juvenile literature. [1. Chemistry.]
I. Grolier Educational (Firm)
QD35.C52 1997
540–dc21   97–23250
                                 CIP
                                 AC

Picture credits
All photographs are from the **Earthscape
Editions** photolibrary except the following:
(c=center t=top b=bottom l=left r=right)
Mary Evans Picture Library 7tr, 8tl, 8br,
9tl, 9cr

*This product is manufactured from sustainable
managed forests. For every tree cut down at least
one more is planted.*

...ts

HOW TO USE THIS BOOK

These two pages show you how to get the most from this book.

❶ THE CONTENTS

Use the table of contents to see how this book is divided into themes. Each theme may have one or more demonstrations.

❷ THEMES

Each theme begins with a theory section on yellow-colored paper. Major themes may contain several pages of theory for the demonstrations that are presented on the subsequent pages. They also contain biographies of scientists whose work was important in the understanding of the theme.

❸ DEMONSTRATIONS

Demonstrations are at the heart of any chemistry study. However, many demonstrations cannot easily be shown to a whole class for health and safety reasons, because the demonstration requires a closeup view, because it is over too quickly, takes too long to complete, or because it requires special apparatus. The demonstrations shown here have been photographed especially to overcome these problems and give you a very closeup view of the key stages in each reaction.

The text, pictures, and diagrams are closely connected. To get the best from the demonstration, look closely at each picture as soon as its reference occurs in the text.

Many of the pictures show enlarged views of parts of the demonstration to help you see exactly what is happening. Notice, too, that most pictures form part of a sequence. You will find that it pays to look at the picture sequence more than once, and always be careful to make sure you can see exactly what is described in any picture before you move on.

The main heading for a demonstration or a set of demonstrations.

An introduction expands on the heading, summarizing the demonstration or group of demonstrations and their context in the theme.

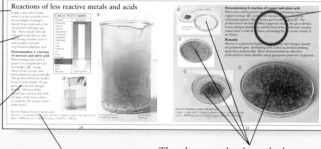

Each demonstration is carefully explained and illustrated with photographs and, where necessary, with diagrams, tables, and graphs. The illustrations referred to are numbered ①, ②, ③, etc.

Chemical equations are shown where appropriate (see the explanation of equations at the bottom of page 5).

The photographs show the key stages that you might see if witnessing a demonstration firsthand. Examine them very carefully against the text description.

APPARATUS

The demonstrations have been carefully conducted as representative examples of the main chemical processes. The apparatus used is standard; but other choices are possible, and you may see different equipment in your laboratory. So make sure you understand the principles behind the apparatus selected. The key pieces of apparatus are defined in the glossary.

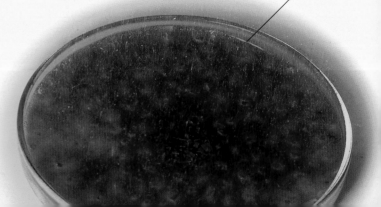

❹ GLOSSARY OF TECHNICAL TERMS

Words with which you may be unfamiliar are shown in small capitals where they first occur in the text. Use the glossary on pages 66–74 to find more information about these technical words. Over four hundred items are presented alphabetically.

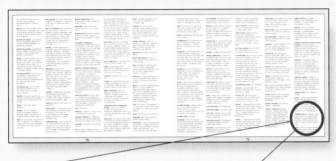

oxidizing agent: a substance that removes electrons from another substance being oxidized (and therefore is itself reduced) in a redox reaction. *Example:* chlorine (Cl₂).

❺ INDEX TO ALL VOLUMES IN THE SET

To look for key words in any of the 12 volumes that make up the ChemLab set, use the Master Index on pages 75 to 80. The instructions on page 75 show you how to cross-reference between volumes.

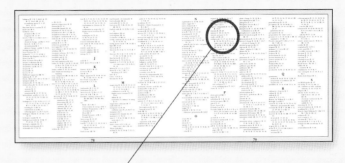

The most important locations of the term "oxidizing agent" are given in a master index that includes references to all of the volumes in the ChemLab set.

ABBREVIATIONS

Units are in the international metric system. Some units of measurement are abbreviated, or shortened, as follows:

$°C$ = degrees Celsius
km = kilometer
m = meter
cm = centimeter
mm = millimeter
sq m = square meter
g = gram
kg = kilogram
kJ = kilojoule
l = liter

❻ CHEMICAL EQUATIONS

Important or relevant chemical equations are shown in written and symbolic form along with additional information.

What the reaction equation illustrates

Word equation

Symbol equation
The symbols for each element can be found in any Periodic Table.

Where relevant, the oxidation state is shown as Roman numerals in parentheses.

EQUATION: Reaction of copper and nitric acid

Copper + nitric acid ⇨ copper(II) nitrate + water + nitrogen dioxide

$Cu(s) + 4HNO_3(conc) ⇨ Cu(NO_3)_2(aq) + 2H_2O(l) + 2NO_2(g)$

Blue

The symbol indicating the state of each substance is shown as follows:
(s) = solid
(g) = gaseous
(l) = liquid
(aq) = aqueous
$(conc)$ = concentrated

The two halves of the chemical equation are separated by the arrow that shows the progression of the reaction. Each side of the equation must balance.

Sometimes additional descriptions are given below the symbol equation.

The correct number of atoms, ions, and molecules and their proportions in any compound are shown by the numbers. A free electron is shown as an e⁻.

AIR

The air is a mixture of gases that together make up the Earth's atmosphere. The most important gases in the atmosphere are nitrogen (N_2, 78% by volume) and oxygen (O_2, 21% by volume).

Although in comparison with these two gases the percentage of all other gases is small, many (such as water vapor, carbon dioxide, sulfur dioxide, and the noble gases, such as helium and argon) do have important influences on the atmosphere or represent valuable resources for the chemist.

The atmosphere of today is probably very different from that in the past. The early atmosphere was most probably dominated by ammonia and methane. It was only when plants began to flourish that oxygen began to become a major part of the air. The amount of argon has gradually increased as part of the natural radioactive decay of the Earth's rocks.

Ozone (O_3, an ALLOTROPE of oxygen) is a rare, but vital, gas. It is found mainly in the upper atmosphere and reaches a maximum concentration of 10 parts per million in the ozone layer at an altitude of 30 kilometers. Ozone is the primary shield for ultraviolet radiation from the Sun.

History of investigations of the air

The constituents of the air have proved difficult to isolate. The ancient scientists were not even able to grasp that the air was a MIXTURE of gases. This was first discovered in the 17th century by John Mayow.

He was able to separate oxygen (because it was used up in COMBUSTION) from all the other gases. However, he was not aware of the nature of the gas he had identified. In fact, it proved easier to work with the part of the air that did not support combustion. Antoine Laurent Lavoisier called it "azote," meaning lifeless, hence explaining the use of the term *azote* by French scientists for the gas called nitrogen in the English language. Daniel Rutherford called it "the poisonous part of the air," although it turned out that

THE PHLOGISTON THEORY

The Phlogiston Theory was an 18th-century way of explaining combustion first introduced by the German scientists Johann Becher and Georg Stahl. This theory suggested that any combustible material contained an invisible substance, phlogiston, which escaped when the material burned.

During the 18th century many famous scientists tried to justify their experimental work using the phlogiston theory.

But it was the French scientist Antoine Lavoisier who began to question it. Lavoisier showed that metals gain weight on burning, while the volume of air becomes smaller by about a fifth.

When Joseph Priestley discovered oxygen (which he called dephlogisticated air), Lavoisier interpreted oxygen as the source of combustion. Lavoisier then found that the compounds formed by burning nonmetals such as sulfur and carbon in oxygen were acidic, and he coined the name oxygen (from the Greek for acid former) for the gas.

Lavoisier also decomposed water by passing it through a hot iron tube. He found that the inside of the tube became coated with rust (iron oxide), while hydrogen gas came out the far end of the tube. This led Lavoisier to propose the name hydrogen (from Greek words meaning water former) for this gas.

As a result of these experiments the phlogiston idea was gradually abandoned.

there was nothing particularly poisonous about any gas in the air.

The first gas to be isolated from the air was one of its minor parts, carbon dioxide. Joseph Black described carbon dioxide (then known as "fixed air") in 1755 and demonstrated that it could be made from DECOMPOSING calcium carbonate. He also showed that calcium carbonate could be made from calcium oxide powder (quicklime) and carbon dioxide gas, thus proving it to be a REVERSIBLE REACTION involving a gas from the air.

Carbon dioxide is absorbed by growing vegetation and by the world's oceans. It is produced by the

(Below) **The composition of clean, dry air by volume.**

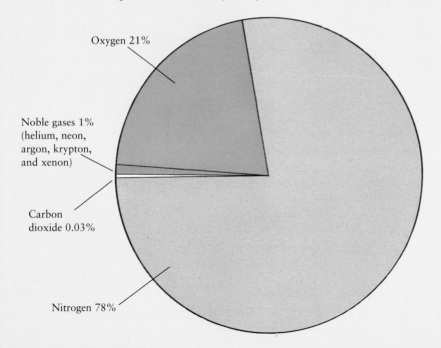

Oxygen 21%

Noble gases 1%
(helium, neon,
argon, krypton,
and xenon)

Carbon
dioxide 0.03%

Nitrogen 78%

GREAT EXPERIMENTAL SCIENTISTS

Joseph Priestley

Joseph Priestley (1733–1804) was born near Leeds, England. He grew up wanting to enter the ministry and remained a dedicated unorthodox Christian believer throughout his life. During his studies in Warrington, England, he met Benjamin Franklin, a colonist from North America. It was Franklin, himself an excellent experimental scientist, who encouraged Priestley on his scientific career. Priestley continued to be interested in electricity and gases, which he described as "different kinds of air."

Priestley lived close to a brewery, and his interest in FERMENTATION led him to study gases more deeply. He found carbon dioxide as a layer of gas that formed over the brewing vat, and which Joseph Black had named "fixed air" just a few years before. He discovered that carbon dioxide would dissolve in water under pressure and give a fizz to water when the pressure was released, thus starting the craze for soda water that continues to this day.

Priestley then moved to Wiltshire, where he invented the pneumatic trough for collecting gases over water. He also collected water-soluble gases over mercury.

His experiments led him to discover nitric oxide (nitrogen monoxide, NO) and then nitrous oxide (dinitrogen oxide, N_2O) in 1772. He then isolated ammonia gas by collecting it over mercury. In 1774–1775 he discovered oxygen by heating mercuric oxide. He called his new gas simply "dephlogisticated air." Thus it was that he told his rival, Antoine Lavoisier, about the experiments, and this encouraged Lavoisier to name the gas oxygen.

Priestley's experiments included the discovery of nine new gases in all, including nitrogen, nitrogen dioxide, hydrogen chloride, and sulfur dioxide.

Priestley continued to be a very controversial religious person, and he was not liked in England for his views against the established church and his support of the French Revolution (which was soon to cost their most famous scientist, Lavoisier, his head). This is why he emigrated to the new United States in 1794, following his three sons, who had gone there earlier. Here, in isolation from controversy, he lived quietly until his death in 1804.

GREAT EXPERIMENTAL SCIENTISTS

John Dalton

John Dalton (1766–1844) was born in Cumberland, England, to Quaker parents. Not being a member of the Church of England, he was not, at that time, allowed to go to Oxford or Cambridge universities. He was bright enough to be a teacher at the age of 12 and later became a headmaster. In 1793 he moved to Manchester, where he taught mathematics. Later he moved to York.

Dalton began collecting meteorological observations in 1787. In 1794 he discovered that he was red-green color blind, a condition that, for a while, become known as Daltonism. He also investigated the change in density of water with temperature.

His meteorological investigations led him to comment: "Having been long accustomed to make meteorological observations, and to speculate upon the nature and constitution of the atmosphere, it often struck me with wonder how a compound atmosphere, or a mixture of two or more elastic fluids, should constitute apparently a homogeneous mass... and thus why the mixture didn't separate out, with the heavier gases sinking to the bottom." This led Dalton to believe that the particles (or ATOMS) of oxygen and nitrogen were of different weight.

Dalton then concluded that mixtures of particles of a gas repel only their own kind and have no effect on particles of other gases. From this he derived his Law of Partial Pressures (that the pressure of the gas equals the pressure of each of the gases present). Later, Dalton went on to propose the Law of Definite Proportions, that is, that elements combine with one another in exactly the same ratio of weights for any given COMPOUND (18 kg of water always contain 16 kg of oxygen and 2 kg of hydrogen).

In 1803 Dalton drew up a table of ATOMIC WEIGHTS, giving hydrogen a value of 1, the beginning of atomic theory. He believed that (i) matter consists of particles called atoms; (ii) that atoms of the same ELEMENT are identical, but that most atoms of different elements have different properties; (iii) when elements combine, they do so in simple proportions to form MOLECULES.

breathing of people and animals and also when natural materials decay or are burned. Carbon dioxide also absorbs heat that would otherwise be lost to space, and for this reason it is often called a "GREENHOUSE GAS."

The discovery and isolation of oxygen was one of the great struggles in scientific history. In the 18th century it was clear that some part of the air was responsible not just for life and combustion but also for rusting and other phenomena. In 1774 Joseph Priestley heated mercury oxide and from it obtained a gas. He was able to show that substances burned better in this new gas (which at the time he thought was phlogiston; see page 6). In 1794 Lavoisier named this new gas oxygen. (Note that oxygen was also discovered independently in 1771 by Karl Scheele in Sweden, but this discovery was not known about in scientific circles until many years later.)

GREAT EXPERIMENTAL SCIENTISTS

James Dewar

Sir James Dewar (1842–1923) was a Scottish scientist who was interested in making gases into liquids. For this purpose he invented a vacuum jacket, called the Dewar Flask, which kept the contents cold. Unfortunately, Dewar didn't patent his invention, and it was later adapted for everyday use and is often known as the "thermos flask."

Dewar was the first person to obtain liquid oxygen, then liquid hydrogen, and finally solid hydrogen. He was also the coinventor of the explosive called cordite.

Great Experimental Scientists

Karl Wilhelm Scheele

Karl Wilhelm Scheele (1742–1786) was born to poor parents in Sweden. At age 14 he was made an apothecary's (pharmacist's) assistant in Gothenburg, and it is at this time that he learned about chemistry. He later became an apothecary in his own right, finally settling in Uppsala, Sweden.

In the 1770s his brilliance as a chemist was recognized, and he was offered many posts in universities; but he preferred to remain an apothecary. Thus it was left to his friends to publicize his work. Nonetheless, he was elected to the Swedish Royal Academy of Science.

Scheele discovered more new substances than anyone else in the history of chemistry. Among the many substances that he discovered, or was connected with discovering, were several elements, including nitrogen and oxygen. He also discovered the effect that light has on silver salts, a vital step in the invention of photography.

However, because he did not move in academic circles and was not intent on publishing his work, other people often got the credit for his discoveries. The classic case of this involved the gas oxygen. Scheele, in fact, discovered oxygen independently and three years before Joseph Priestley (to whom the discovery is popularly attributed).

Scheele got all of his extensive experimental work into a short life, dying when he was only 43.

Gradually, it became possible to isolate all of the gases in the air. By 1784 Henry Cavendish had accurately determined the percentages of nitrogen and oxygen by volume in the air. The other main gas, argon, was inert. Cavendish knew it was inert but was unable to identify it. This was finally achieved in 1894 by Lord Rayleigh and Sir William Ramsay.

Great Experimental Scientists

Henry Cavendish

Henry Cavendish (1731–1810) was an extremely wealthy man, a recluse, and a famous English scientist. He went to Cambridge University but left without earning a degree. His father encouraged his scientific interests, and he was thus able to perform experiments at will.

Cavendish spent much of his time studying gases and was the first to demonstrate that hydrogen, which he called "inflammable air," existed as a gas separately from carbon dioxide, known as "fixed air."

He studied the solution of metals in natural water supplies and thus discovered hard water and calcium carbonate.

By putting a mixture of hydrogen and oxygen into a narrow glass tube and introducing an electric spark, he obtained an explosion that yielded water droplets, thus showing that water was a compound of these two gases. At the same time, he showed that the gases were reduced in volume. He also showed that nitric acid was a mixture of nitrogen, oxygen, and water vapor.

From all of these investigations he deduced that air is four-fifths nitrogen and one-fifth oxygen.

Cavendish believed that every charged body was surrounded by an electric atmosphere, and this eventually helped in the formulation of the theory of electrical fields and the nature of static electricity.

The Cavendish Laboratory in Cambridge, England, one of the foremost research institutions in the world, is named after him.

Demonstrating that air contains oxygen

There are many ways of demonstrating that air contains oxygen, several of them connected with the way that oxygen from the air is used up during combustion. This demonstration uses white phosphorus.

Demonstration: combustion of phosphorus in air

White phosphorus is an extremely reactive element of Group 5 in the PERIODIC TABLE. This particular form of phosphorus is very unstable because of the arrangement of the phosphorus atom.

White phosphorus is supplied as sticks for use in the laboratory, and because it is really quite soft, it can be cut with a spatula (①). However, even chopping a small piece off a stick causes the freshly cut end to smoke. Since phosphorus can spontaneously ignite before it is replaced under water, some speed is useful when handling it in air.

The apparatus used in this demonstration consists of a bell jar and a pneumatic trough containing water (②). If some Universal Indicator is added to the tap water in the trough and stirred, the resulting solution becomes slightly purple.

Universal Indicator

Bell jar with stopper

Tap water and Universal Indicator

Pneumatic trough

White phosphorus stored under water

Crucible lid floated on a cork

White phosphorus

Cutting white phosphorus with a spatula

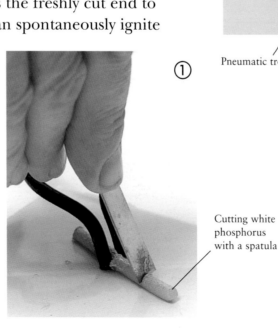

The presence of the indicator helps show what is happening during the combustion reaction.

A small piece of phosphorus is to be floated on, but kept out of contact with, the water inside the bell jar. To do this, a float is made out of a crucible lid fixed to a cork.

The piece of phosphorus is placed on the crucible lid (③) and the bell jar placed over the top, first removing the stopper so that the water levels inside and outside the jar can become the same. To speed up the start of combustion, the phosphorus is touched with a warm piece of wire through the top of the bell jar (④) and the stopper quickly put back (⑤).

Combustion of the phosphorus rapidly uses up the oxygen in the bell jar and produces a white smoke of

④

Wire with heated tip is used to ignite phosphorus.

EQUATION: Phosphorus burns to produce acidic phosphorus(V) oxide
Phosphorus + oxygen ⇨ phosphorus(V) oxide
$P_4(s, white) + 5O_2(g) ⇨ P_4O_{10}(s)$

⑤

Bell jar containing air is sealed with a large stopper.

Phosphorus(V) oxide smoke

phosphoric oxide particles (⑥). At first, the heat from the burning phosphorus will make the gas inside the bell jar expand, and so the water level will fall inside the bell jar and rise in the trough (⑦). However, as the oxygen is used up, the burning stops, the gas inside the bell jar cools down, and the level of water inside the bell jar starts to rise.

The white phosphorus oxide will settle either on the sides of the gas jar or on the water. As this happens, the color of the indicator inside the bell jar will turn to red as the phosphorus(V) oxide combines with water to form phosphoric acid. The product of the combustion of phosphorus in air is therefore an acidic oxide.

The rise in water level inside the bell jar is a rough guide to the proportion of the air, and therefore oxygen, used during the combustion (⑧).

Remarks

White phosphorus is normally kept under water because exposure to air leads to SPONTANEOUS COMBUSTION.

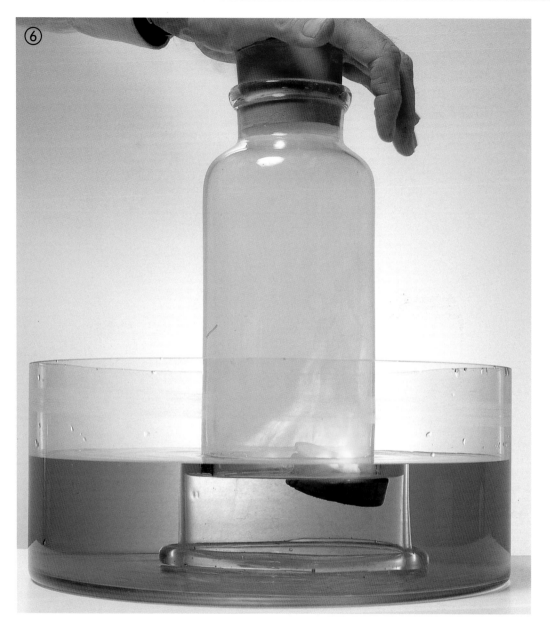

⑦

⑧

The water level rises, showing the proportion of oxygen in the air in the gas jar.

The phosphorus(V) oxide dissolves in the water, forming phosphoric acid, which turns the indicator red.

Calculating the percentage by volume of oxygen in the air

Air consists of a mixture of gases dominated by nitrogen and oxygen. One way of determining the percentage of oxygen in air is to remove the oxygen by a chemical (OXIDATION) reaction and note the change in volume of the air. This was done in an approximate, but rapid, way on page 10. In the following demonstrations the percentage of oxygen is determined more accurately using slower forms of oxidation.

Demonstration 1: oxidizing phosphorus slowly in air

The apparatus consists of a long, narrow, graduated tube, a gas jar, and a piece of phosphorus on the end of a wire.

First, a small amount of phosphorus is melted under water in a test tube and the hooked wire inserted. As the phosphorus cools, it solidifies around the wire (①), thus allowing the wire and phosphorus to be taken out of the test tube. During heating the water prevents ignition.

The phosphorus has to be exposed to a known volume of air.

The wire and phosphorus are now inserted into the inverted graduated tube (②). The tube has enough water in it so that when it is turned the right way up and placed in the gas jar containing water, the levels can be adjusted so that the water in the tube and the gas jar are the same (that is, the gas in the tube is at atmospheric pressure). In this demonstration the graduated tube is adjusted to contain about 50 cm^3 of trapped air (③).

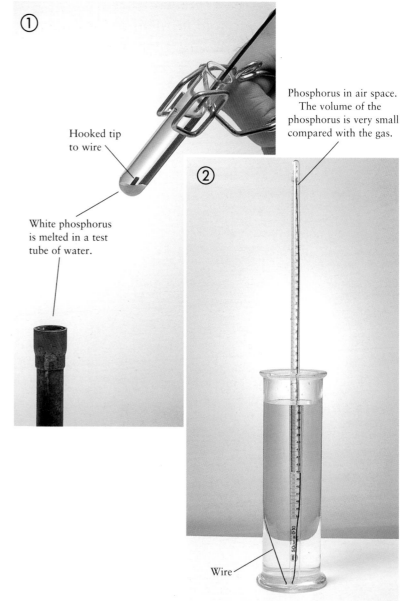

①

Hooked tip to wire

White phosphorus is melted in a test tube of water.

Phosphorus in air space. The volume of the phosphorus is very small compared with the gas.

②

Wire

The graduated tube is then clamped and the apparatus left undisturbed for 2 to 3 months. The phosphorus will react with, and remove, the oxygen from the known volume of air to form solid phosphorus(V) oxide. The change in the volume of the air is a measure of the proportion of oxygen.

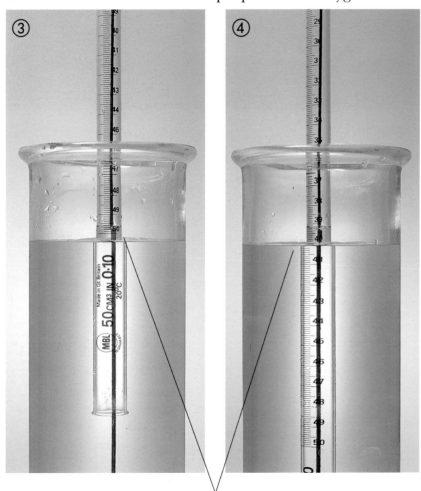

Water levels are adjusted to be the same inside and outside, and then the volume is read from the measuring tube.

Periodically, the level of water in the tube is adjusted to match the level in the gas jar and so bring the gas back to ATMOSPHERIC PRESSURE. The new volume is then recorded. When the volume ceases to change between readings, the final volume has been achieved, and all the oxygen in the air sample has reacted with the phosphorus. In this demonstration the initial volume was 50 cm^3, and the final volume was about 39 cm^3 (④). Thus 11 cm^3 of oxygen were used up. This is, of course, approximately 21% of the original air volume, the percentage of oxygen by volume generally present in air.

Remarks

In order to read the volume of gas in the tube, it is important to make sure that the pressure on the gas is always the same. This is why the tube is raised and lowered until the water level inside the tube is the same as the level outside. Furthermore, readings should only be taken when the atmospheric pressure is the same as when the apparatus was set up. It is therefore important to note the atmospheric pressure using a barometer and only make readings when the atmospheric pressure is the same as when the first reading was taken. This will then constitute a fair test of the volume of gas consumed.

Note that the photograph has been taken before the levels in the tube and the gas jar have been adjusted in order to make it possible to see the water in the tube.

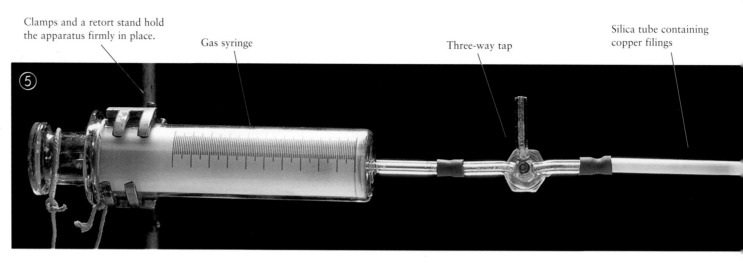

Clamps and a retort stand hold the apparatus firmly in place.

Gas syringe

Three-way tap

Silica tube containing copper filings

⑤

Demonstration 2: oxidizing copper in air

As an alternative to slow oxidation at room temperature, a metal can be oxidized by heating it in a closed system that contains a known amount of air. If a surplus of metal is used, then the reaction between the metal and the oxygen in the air will use up all the oxygen in the air, and so the amount of gas left in the system will get smaller.

The apparatus consists of two gas syringes joined together with a three-way tap and a heat-resistant silica tube. The apparatus is clamped between two retort stands in a horizontal position (⑤).

A gas syringe is similar to a hyperdermic syringe in that it contains a piston that runs in and out of a glass cylinder. The piston is precision-ground so that it is a gas-tight fit into the cylinder. The sides of the cylinder are marked off in graduations to enable changes in gas volume to be measured.

The other specialized piece of equipment is a silica tube. Silica has a low coefficient of expansion

(which means it is not very likely to crack when heated) and a high melting point (which means it can be used as a minifurnace).

The silica tube is packed with copper filings (small shavings of copper). One end of the tube is connected to a three-way tap. The tap allows air to be expelled or admitted into the syringe-tube system.

The tap is turned to allow air to enter the syringe on the left nearest the tap. The syringe is now pushed in fully to expel the air. (The three-way tap is turned to connect the tube and the other syringe, and this syringe pulled out until it reads 50 cm^3 (⑤ again).) The three-way tap is now turned again so that it connects both syringes, but so that it isolates the apparatus from the atmosphere.

The silica tube and copper filings are now heated in a Bunsen flame until the reaction produces solid, black copper oxide (⑥). Using the two syringes, the trapped air can now be pushed backward and forward

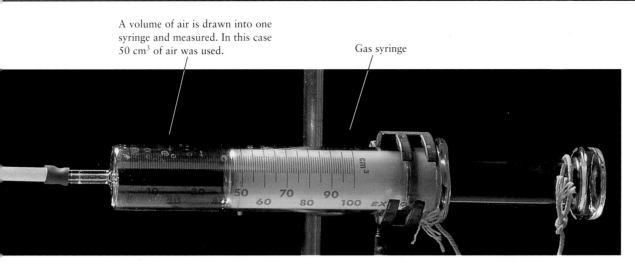

A volume of air is drawn into one syringe and measured. In this case 50 cm³ of air was used.

Gas syringe

EQUATION: Oxidation of copper
Copper + oxygen ⇨ copper(II) oxide
$2Cu(s) + O_2(g) \Rightarrow 2CuO(s)$

through the silica tube and over the copper filings (⑦). The copper oxide occupies hardly any more volume than the original copper filings.

For small quantities of air, heating the copper for five minutes is sufficient to use up all of the oxygen. The heat is then removed, and the apparatus is allowed to cool down. The syringe now reads about 40 cm³ instead of its starting value of 50 cm³. About 10 cm³, or 20%, of the air has been consumed in the oxidation of the copper. This is a measurement of the proportion of oxygen in the air sample.

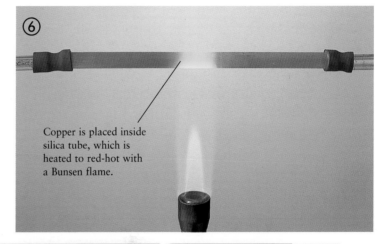

⑥

Copper is placed inside silica tube, which is heated to red-hot with a Bunsen flame.

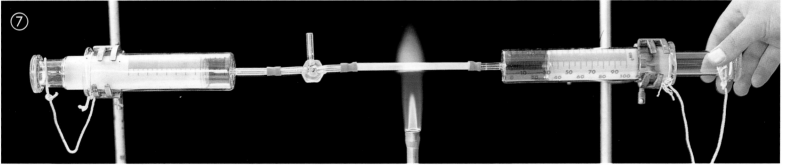

⑦

Testing for nitrogen in the air

Although nitrogen makes up almost four-fifths of the atmosphere, it is difficult to test for nitrogen gas because it is a very unreactive element. However, when magnesium burns in air, so much energy is liberated that nitrogen also reacts with the magnesium to form a solid, magnesium nitride. This is contained in the white, solid ash that is the product of the combustion.

Demonstration: combustion of magnesium in air

The apparatus uses a crucible and lid. The objective is to heat the crucible with magnesium inside it until it turns into magnesium oxide. To ensure the magnesium oxidizes, it is important to use a loose-fitting lid to the crucible so that air can enter.

A strip of magnesium ribbon is placed inside the crucible. The crucible containing the magnesium strip is placed on a pipe-clay triangle on the tripod, and the lid is placed on top (①). The crucible and its contents are heated over an intense Bunsen flame until it glows red-hot (②).

During the heating the magnesium reacts with the oxygen in the air to form magnesium oxide (MgO). However, it also reacts with nitrogen in the air to form magnesium nitride (Mg_3N_2).

To prove that the crucible contains nitride, the crucible is allowed to cool and the lid removed (③). Distilled water is now added. The magnesium nitride reacts with the water to form magnesium hydroxide, and at the same time it gives off ammonia gas.

The presence of the gas can be tested for with damp pH paper (④) – it turns the pH paper blue because ammonia is an alkaline gas (⑤).

EQUATION: **Combustion reaction of magnesium with the oxygen in air**
Magnesium + oxygen ⇨ magnesium oxide
$2Mg(s) + O_2(g) ⇨ 2MgO(s)$

EQUATION: **Combustion reaction of magnesium with the nitrogen in air**
Magnesium + nitrogen ⇨ magnesium nitride
$3Mg(s) + N_2(g) ⇨ Mg_3N_2(s)$

EQUATION: **Adding water to the combustion product**
Magnesium nitride + water ⇨ magnesium hydroxide + ammonia gas
$Mg_3N_2(s) + 6H_2O(l) ⇨ 3Mg(OH)_2(aq) + 2NH_3(g)$

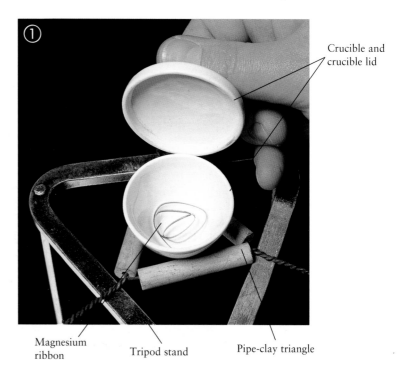

① Crucible and crucible lid

Magnesium ribbon

Tripod stand

Pipe-clay triangle

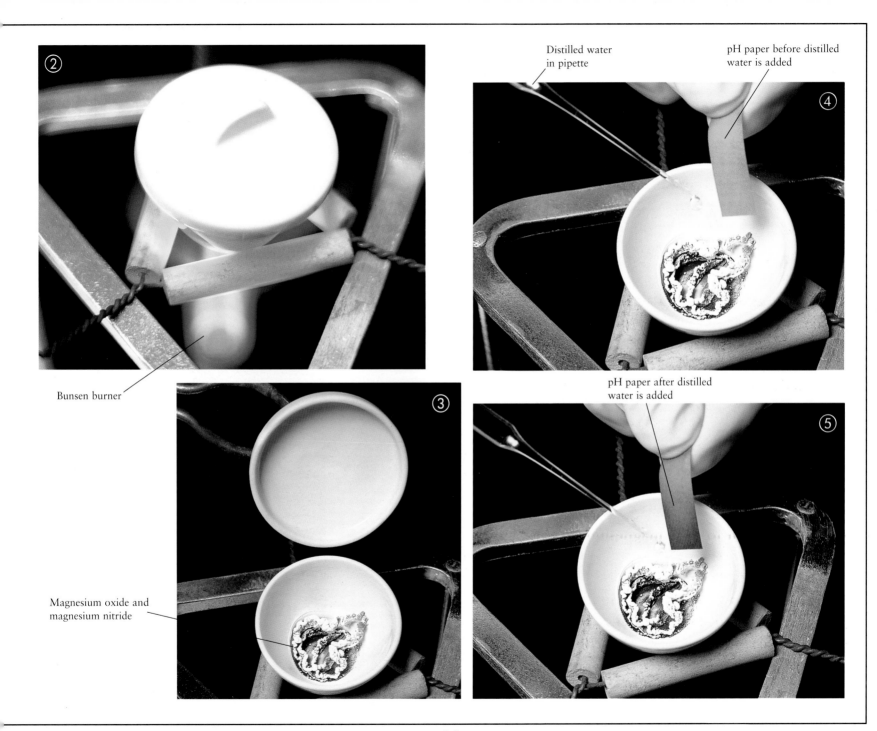

② Bunsen burner

③ Magnesium oxide and magnesium nitride

④ Distilled water in pipette

pH paper before distilled water is added

⑤ pH paper after distilled water is added

Testing for carbon dioxide in the air

Carbon dioxide exists as a very small proportion (0.03%) of the atmosphere, but its presence can be detected readily. This can be done either by bubbling air through limewater, or by noticing its reaction with sodium hydroxide. In both cases the metals are SPECTATOR IONS, the active reaction being the combining of a hydroxide with carbon dioxide to form a carbonate.

Demonstration 1: reacting carbon dioxide and air with sodium hydroxide

First, we need to establish that carbon dioxide will react with sodium hydroxide to form a white precipitate.

A Petri dish is half filled with sodium hydroxide solution, and a funnel is inverted (①) and placed in the liquid (②). The funnel is connected to a supply of laboratory-produced carbon dioxide (for example, a KIPP'S APPARATUS or a flask, used to react hydrochloric acid with calcium carbonate). The purpose of the funnel is to produce a large surface area for reaction between the gas and the liquid.

After carbon dioxide had been allowed to bubble through the solution for a while, the supply of carbon

Funnel

Petri dish

Colorless sodium hydroxide

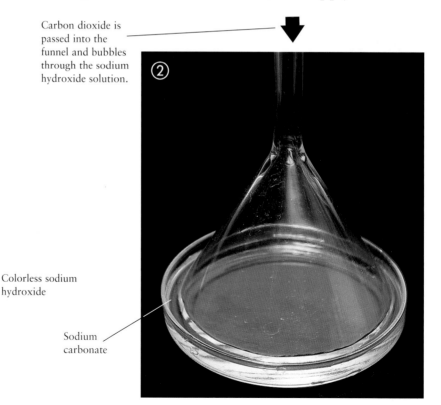

Carbon dioxide is passed into the funnel and bubbles through the sodium hydroxide solution.

②

Sodium carbonate

dioxide was turned off, the funnel lifted slightly clear of the sodium hydroxide solution, and the apparatus left overnight. The following morning a white encrustation of sodium carbonate was found on the rim of the funnel and across the Petri dish (③).

What happens overnight is that the reaction first produces colorless hydrated crystals of sodium

EQUATION: reaction of carbon dioxide with sodium hydroxide
Carbon dioxide + sodium hydroxide ⇨ sodium carbonate + water
$CO_2(g) + 2NaOH(aq) ⇨ Na_2CO_3(s) + H_2O(l)$

③

Sodium carbonate
encrustation

carbonate, but overnight these EFFLORESCE (dehydrate in air), changing to a white powder.

The equivalent demonstration using the carbon dioxide in the air can now be performed. All that is required is a glass reagent bottle and a stopper. Fill the reagent bottle with sodium hydroxide, shake it, and then leave it in air for a week. At the end of this time the stopper will be encrusted with a white deposit of sodium carbonate, since the carbon dioxide has reacted with the sodium hydroxide from the bottle (④).

Remarks

If the stoppers on sodium hydroxide bottles are left undisturbed for too long, the chances are that the growth of the sodium carbonate deposit will cement the stopper firmly to the bottle! This is the reason why sodium hydroxide bottles are fitted with rubber or plastic stoppers. A plastic stopper is flexible enough to be worked clear of the glass.

④

Sodium carbonate
encrustation

Demonstration 2: reacting air with calcium hydroxide

This demonstration will also test for the presence of carbon dioxide in the air. It consists of a side-arm boiling tube partly filled with calcium hydroxide solution (limewater) (⑤) and fitted with an inlet tube that leads through the stopper into the calcium hydroxide solution. A rubber tube is connected from the side arm to a suction pump.

The suction pump is switched on (⑥). As the demonstration proceeds, air is sucked through the calcium hydroxide by the pump. The passage of the air is shown as it bubbles through the solution. Because the carbon dioxide is a small part of the atmosphere, it takes about a day for the limewater to turn cloudy (⑦).

Remarks

The time taken for the calcium hydroxide to detect carbon dioxide in the air depends on the rate at which air can be drawn through the solution, and this varies with the equipment used. If carbon dioxide is bubbled through calcium hydroxide for too long, the cloudiness will disappear, and the solution will turn clear again. Thus one day is probably the right length of time for the demonstration to run, whereas three days would be too long. It is desirable to check the apparatus daily to find when the cloudiness is most intense.

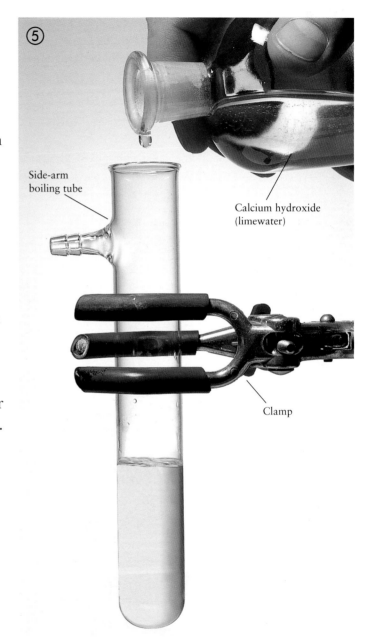

⑤

Side-arm boiling tube

Calcium hydroxide (limewater)

Clamp

EQUATION 1: Initial reaction of carbon dioxide with calcium hydroxide
Carbon dioxide + calcium hydroxide ⇨ calcium carbonate + water
$CO_2(g) + Ca(OH)_2(aq)$ ⇨ $CaCO_3(s) + H_2O(l)$

EQUATION 2: Prolonged reaction of carbon dioxide with calcium hydroxide
Carbon dioxide + calcium carbonate + water ⇨ calcium hydrogen carbonate
$CO_2(g) + CaCO_3(s) + H_2O(l)$ ⇨ $Ca(HCO_3)_2(aq)$

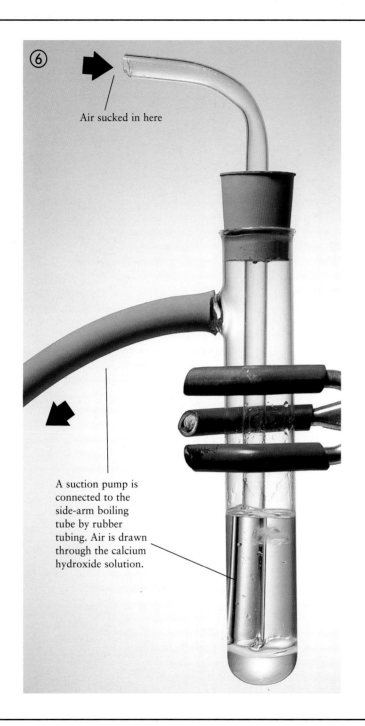

⑥ **Air sucked in here**

A suction pump is connected to the side-arm boiling tube by rubber tubing. Air is drawn through the calcium hydroxide solution.

⑦

Cloudiness from the calcium carbonate particles in solution

WATER

Water is one of the main constituents of the surface of the Earth. It is present as salt water in the Earth's oceans and found as fresh water in rivers, lakes, and the world's ice sheets and glaciers. A small, but vital, percentage of the world's water is found as vapor in the atmosphere.

Water is useful in the chemist's laboratory. It is a REACTANT and also an excellent SOLVENT and a CATALYST for many chemical reactions.

Water molecules

Many of the properties of water result from its very unusual structure. Water MOLECULES consist of two hydrogen ATOMS and one oxygen atom (H_2O) BONDED at an angle of about 104 degrees (①). The hydrogen atoms are attached to the oxygen by COVALENT BONDS.

One important property of a water molecule is that it is highly POLAR. This means that it behaves as though it has a positive charge at one end and a negative charge at the other. The poles are found at the oxygen atom (which has a net negative charge) and midway between the hydrogen atoms (which have a net positive charge). This polar property is produced from the bent shape of the molecule. The polarity can be demonstrated by charging up a plastic comb with static electricity (rubbing it against clothing) and then placing it close to a thin stream of water flowing from a tap. The stream of water will bend toward the comb, attracted by static electricity.

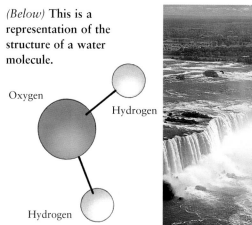

(Below) This is a representation of the structure of a water molecule.

Oxygen

Hydrogen

Hydrogen

Ice, the solid form of water, forms in eight different structures. Each water molecule of an ice crystal (which may accumulate to form a snowflake) is bonded to its neighbors by weak HYDROGEN BONDS.

Hydrogen bonding of water molecules gives water many properties quite unlike any other substance. It accounts for the surface tension effect in water as well as melting and boiling points higher than would be expected by comparing water with other substances.

For example, when water freezes into ice, hydrogen bonding holds the water molecules apart in a LATTICE that makes ice only nine-tenths as dense as liquid water (②). There are far more hydrogen bonds in ice than in liquid water, and as melting occurs, some of the hydrogen bonds break, allowing water molecules to pack together more closely and making liquid water much denser than the solid.

The gaseous form of water is called water vapor. Steam is water vapor produced as the result of boiling, but evaporation will provide enough energy to allow water to evaporate throughout its liquid range. Unlike liquid water and ice, in which the water molecules are bonded together, water vapor consists of individual molecules.

Chemical properties of water

Covalent water molecules make water a very poor conductor of electricity. But at the same time, water is an excellent solvent, and many substances that are IONIC will dissolve in it. This works because the water dramatically reduces the attractive forces between the CATIONS and ANIONS of a substance and allows them to break apart.

Any substance dissolved in water is called an AQUEOUS SOLUTION (a solution in water). Once a substance has become ionized in water, the conductivity of the aqueous solution increases dramatically. Thus it is only distilled water that is a good insulator; normal tap water contains many dissolved salts and so is a relatively good conductor of electricity.

Water is a stable substance and will not DISSOCIATE into hydrogen and oxygen gases unless a large amount of energy is applied, for example, in the form of an electric current (see page 32). Thus boiling water will not make it dissociate; it merely makes it turn into a vapor.

Water can act either as an OXIDIZING AGENT or as a REDUCING AGENT. For example, water can oxidize carbon to carbon monoxide (page 54), liberating hydrogen gas. It can also reduce chlorine gas to hydrogen chloride, releasing oxygen gas (page 56).

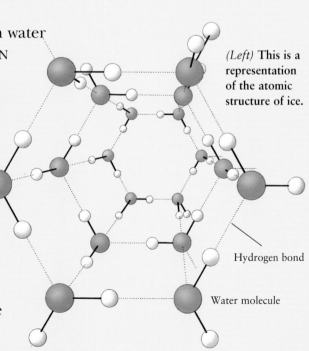

(Left) **This is a representation of the atomic structure of ice.**

Hydrogen bond

Water molecule

Testing for liquid water

The two common tests for the presence of water in a liquid are that it turns:

(a) anhydrous cobalt(II) chloride pink.

(b) anhydrous copper(II) sulfate blue.

However, because any liquid *containing* water will pass both of these tests, the only test that will verify that a colorless solution is pure water is to check that its boiling point is 100°C and its freezing point 0°C.

Demonstration 1: using anhydrous cobalt(II) chloride

Cobalt chloride is the most sensitive of the indicators for water. If left out in a room for a while, the water vapor in the air will be sufficient to turn it pink. In the demonstration below a few drops of water were added to purplish-blue–colored cobalt(II) chloride powder on a watch glass (①). The color change to pink occurred within a few seconds (② & ③) (an example of the use of this test is shown on page 30).

① Distilled water is added from a pipette.

Purplish-blue anhydrous cobalt(II) chloride

②

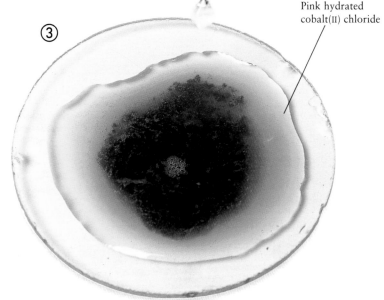

③

Pink hydrated cobalt(II) chloride

EQUATION: Test for water using cobalt(II) chloride

Anhydrous cobalt(II) chloride + water ⇨ hydrated cobalt(II) chloride

$CoCl_2(s) + 6H_2O(l) \Rightarrow CoCl_2 \bullet 6H_2O(s)$

Blue solid   Pink solid

Demonstration 2: using anhydrous copper(II) sulfate

Anhydrous copper(II) sulfate is a white powder. It is more stable in air than cobalt(II) chloride and is often used as a drying agent in demonstrations. When a few drops of water are added to some white anhydrous copper(II) sulfate powder on a watch glass (③), the powder turns blue as the water is absorbed into the structure of the copper(II) sulfate (④ & ⑤) (see page 36).

⑥

Blue hydrated copper(II) sulfate

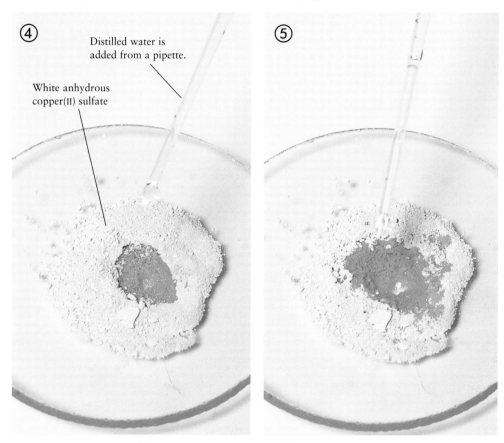

④

Distilled water is added from a pipette.

White anhydrous copper(II) sulfate

⑤

EQUATION: Test for water using copper(II) sulfate
Anhydrous copper(II) sulfate + water ⇨ hydrated copper(II) sulfate
$CuSO_4(s) + 5H_2O(l) ⇨ CuSO_4 \bullet 5H_2O(s)$
White solid   Blue solid

Testing for water vapor in air

The presence of water vapor in the air can be shown in many ways. Here are a variety of demonstrations from the purely observational to the more chemically complex.

Demonstration 1: observing boiling water

When water is boiled, it gives off invisible water vapor (①). However, the amount of water vapor that can be contained in air is limited, and in cool conditions the water vapor recondenses to form droplets. The effect is to produce steam, as seen, for example, with a boiling kettle.

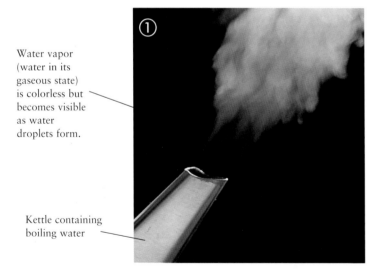

Water vapor (water in its gaseous state) is colorless but becomes visible as water droplets form.

Kettle containing boiling water

Demonstration 2: observing freezing water

The fact that water vapor exists in the air can be demonstrated by freezing a bottle and then exposing it to the air (②). The cold surface of the bottle cools down the surrounding air, and the amount of water vapor the air can hold is reduced. The surplus water condenses and then freezes on the bottle surface as an icy coating.

Demonstration 3: hydration of concentrated sulfuric acid

Concentrated sulfuric acid has a strong affinity for water and will absorb it from the air to make a more dilute solution of the acid, becoming progressively more HYDRATED. This can be used to show the presence of water vapor in the air because, over time, the volume of very concentrated sulfuric acid exposed to air will increase as it absorbs water.

To demonstrate this property, two bottles (③), one half filled with water and the other containing an equal volume of concentrated sulfuric acid (yellow dye was added to identify the acid), are placed inside an airtight container (④). Over the following weeks the concentrated sulfuric acid takes the water out of the air and becomes more dilute. Evaporation occurs from the bottle containing the water, and this water vapor is also absorbed by the concentrated acid. As a result, the level of liquid in the acid bottle rises, and the acid becomes more dilute, while the level in the water bottle falls (⑤).

As the water froze in the bottle, it expanded, cracking the glass.

③

Distilled water Concentrated sulfuric acid

④

Airtight container Bottles left open

⑤

Evaporation of water Hydration of sulfuric acid

Combustion of hydrogen to form water

Water can be produced by reacting hydrogen with oxygen in the air.

Demonstration: burning dry hydrogen in air

In this demonstration dry hydrogen is burned in air and the products of the reaction tested for water using anhydrous cobalt(II) chloride (①, see also page 34).

A supply of hydrogen is generated in a flask by reacting dilute hydrochloric acid (containing a copper catalyst) and zinc. Some steam is produced during this reaction, and so the hydrogen is dried by passing it over calcium chloride granules in a U-shaped tube.

The dry hydrogen burns with a colorless flame. But because of the high temperature of the flame, it also melts some of the glass nozzle, and the sodium content masks the hydrogen color and instead shows the color of heated sodium, which is yellow (②).

The gas from the combustion of hydrogen in air is collected in a wide-necked vessel (③). Condensation is seen in the vessel; but to prove this is indeed water, the combustion products are sucked into a side-arm boiling tube containing blue cobalt(II) chloride using a suction pump. Water vapor turns cobalt(II) chloride

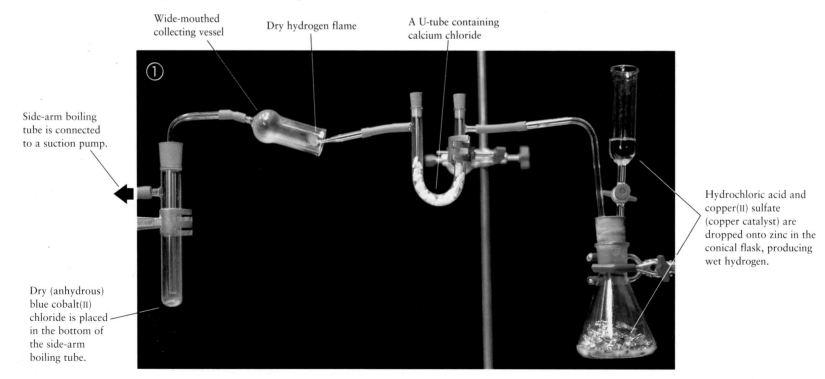

Wide-mouthed collecting vessel

Dry hydrogen flame

A U-tube containing calcium chloride

Side-arm boiling tube is connected to a suction pump.

Dry (anhydrous) blue cobalt(II) chloride is placed in the bottom of the side-arm boiling tube.

Hydrochloric acid and copper(II) sulfate (copper catalyst) are dropped onto zinc in the conical flask, producing wet hydrogen.

①

pink (④), showing that the combustion does, indeed, produce water.

Remarks

An alternative, and simpler, demonstration can be done by playing the dry hydrogen flame onto a flask containing cold water. The combustion of the hydrogen in air produces water vapor, which then condenses on the cold surface of the flask (⑤).

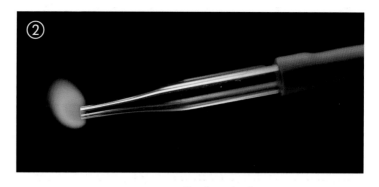

Condensation in collecting tube

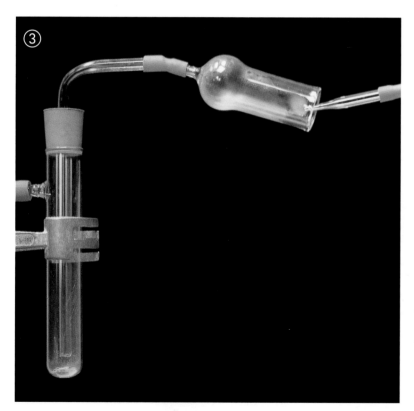

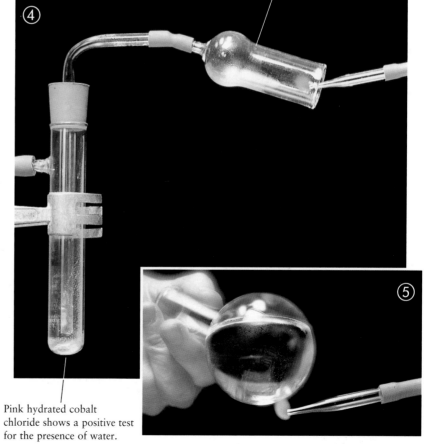

Pink hydrated cobalt chloride shows a positive test for the presence of water.

EQUATION: Combustion of hydrogen with oxygen

Hydrogen + oxygen ⇨ water

$2H_2(g) + O_2(g) ⇨ 2H_2O(aq)$

Decomposing water by electrolysis

Water can be decomposed by an electrical current. This process is called ELECTROLYSIS. Electricity is an important source of energy for many chemical reactions. Pure water is not a good ELECTROLYTE, but it can be made to contain sufficient IONS by the use of a solute such as sodium sulfate. Neither the sodium nor the sulfate ions yield gases, so the only gases evolved are from the ionization of water.

Demonstration: electrolysis of a sodium sulfate solution in water

This apparatus is suitable for carrying out electrolysis in which gases are liberated. A platinum (nonreacting) ELECTRODE, held by a rubber stopper, is placed in each arm of a U-tube containing an aqueous solution of sodium sulfate (①). Sodium sulfate is colorless, and so, to provide visual information about the progress of the reaction, some Universal Indicator is added (②). The indicator is green initially, showing that the solution is neutral.

The electrodes are connected to a power pack by cables and crocodile clips. The side arms of the U-tube allow the gases produced in the space above the solution to be led off for collection. The gases are collected over water in two inverted boiling tubes,

ELECTROCHEMICAL REACTIONS AND ELECTROLYSIS

There are two kinds of electrochemical reactions: those that occur when electricity flows through a substance and those reactions that produce electricity (batteries). Both rely on a liquid chemical medium in which ions can move freely. This liquid is called an ELECTROLYTE. It will conduct an electric current while, at the same time, being chemically changed or decomposed by the current. Chemists call the container that holds the electrolyte a CELL.

In an ELECTROLYTIC CELL electricity from an outside power source such as a battery or power supply is passed through the electrolyte using conductors called ELECTRODES. The electrode connected to the positive terminal of the battery is called an ANODE, and the electrode connected to the negative terminal of the battery is called a CATHODE.

An electrolyte conducts electricity because it contains a SOLVENT, such as water, and a SOLUTE that ionizes (splits apart into positively charged ions — cations — and negatively charged ions — anions. For example, sulfuric acid (the solute) dissolves in water (the solvent) to make an aqueous (in water) solution containing positively charged hydrogen ions (H^+, cations) and negatively charged sulfate ions (SO_4^-, anions). Some of the water also dissociates into H^+ and OH^- ions.

Because the solute consists of charged ions, the positive (anode) of the cell attracts the negative (in the case of this example sulfate and hydroxide) anions. When the anions reach the anode, they give up electrons and thus discharge (lose their charge). The hydroxide ions form (oxygen) atoms, which may then group themselves into molecules (in this case of oxygen gas). The cations (in the case of this example hydrogen ions) are attracted to the negative electrode (cathode) of the cell, where they gain electrons and thus discharge (lose their charge) and form (hydrogen) atoms, which then produce hydrogen gas at the cathode. The decomposition of an electrolyte using electricity is called ELECTROLYSIS.

The founder of electrochemistry
The English scientist Michael Faraday established the laws governing electrochemical behavior in the middle of the 19th century. He concluded that the amount of an element liberated by a specific quantity of electricity is related to the atomic weight of the element. For example, the same amount of electricity that will produce 1 gram of hydrogen will produce 16 grams of oxygen. It was Faraday who also introduced the terms electrode, anode, cathode, ion, anion, and cation.

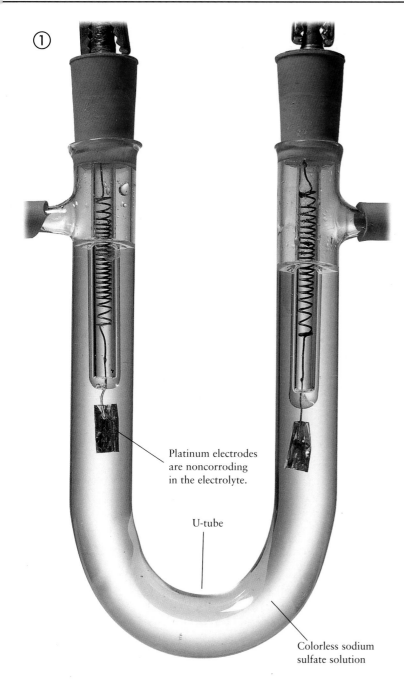

①

Platinum electrodes
are noncorroding
in the electrolyte.

U-tube

Colorless sodium
sulfate solution

each filled with water. These are suspended in small pneumatic troughs by means of clamps.

As the electric current is applied to the solution, gas is liberated at the electrodes. In this demonstration hydrogen is liberated at the CATHODE (negative terminal), which in this case is on the left, and oxygen is liberated at the ANODE (positive terminal) on the right (③, see page 34).

At the same time as the gases are generated, the indicator changes color at the electrodes: violet at one and red at the other, indicating an acid reaction at one electrode (red) and an alkaline reaction at the other electrode (violet) (④, ⑤ & ⑥, see pages 34 and 35).

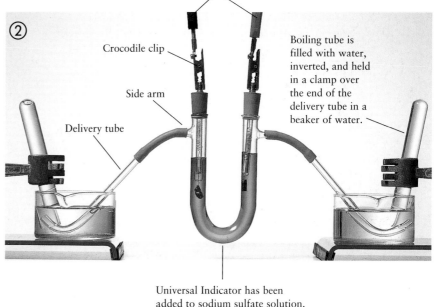

A power pack supplies an electrical current that is passed through the sodium sulfate solution (electrolyte) via the electrodes.

②

Crocodile clip

Boiling tube is filled with water, inverted, and held in a clamp over the end of the delivery tube in a beaker of water.

Side arm

Delivery tube

Universal Indicator has been added to sodium sulfate solution.

During the demonstration gas is released vigorously from both electrodes. Notice that as the gases accumulate, twice the volume of hydrogen gas is given off as oxygen gas, thus verifying the formula for water as H_2O (two hydrogen atoms to every oxygen atom).

The presence of hydrogen and oxygen can be tested. To test for hydrogen, the left-hand boiling tube is lifted clear of the water, while the end is sealed to prevent the gas escaping. A lighted splint is put into the tube. Immediately, there is a loud, high-pitched, popping sound indicating the presence of inflammable hydrogen. To test for oxygen, the right-hand boiling tube is lifted clear of the water. A glowing (not lighted) splint is applied to the mouth of the tube, and it is immediately rekindled, a positive test for oxygen.

④

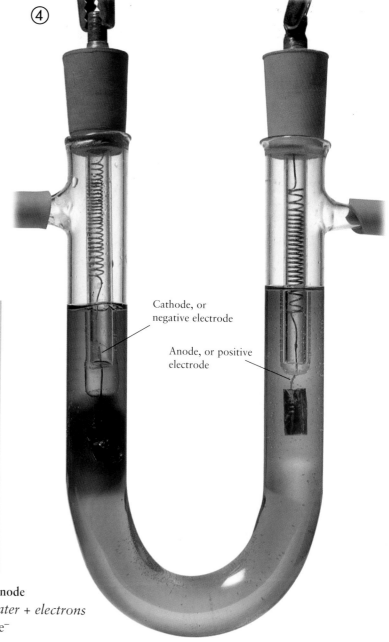

Cathode, or negative electrode

Anode, or positive electrode

③

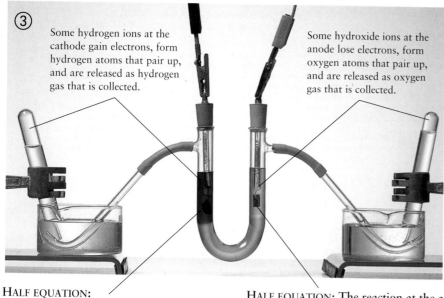

Some hydrogen ions at the cathode gain electrons, form hydrogen atoms that pair up, and are released as hydrogen gas that is collected.

Some hydroxide ions at the anode lose electrons, form oxygen atoms that pair up, and are released as oxygen gas that is collected.

HALF EQUATION:
The reaction at the cathode
Hydrogen ions ⇨ hydrogen
$2H^+(aq) + 2e^- \Rightarrow H_2(g)$
Electric current

HALF EQUATION: The reaction at the anode
Hydroxide ions ⇨ oxygen gas + water + electrons
$4OH^-(aq) \Rightarrow O_2(g) + 2H_2O(l) + 4e^-$
Electric current

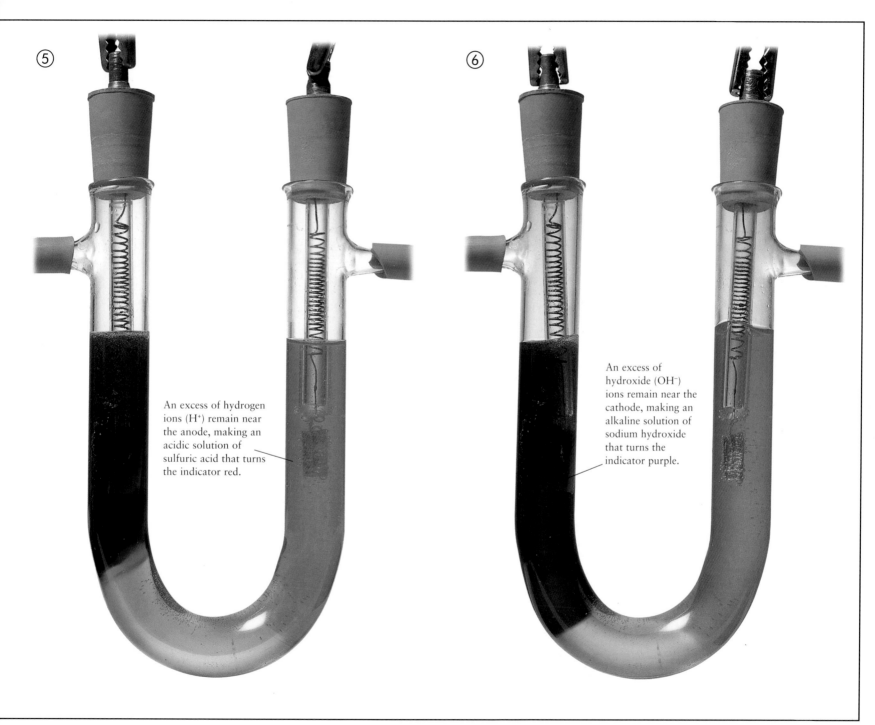

⑤

An excess of hydrogen ions (H⁺) remain near the anode, making an acidic solution of sulfuric acid that turns the indicator red.

⑥

An excess of hydroxide (OH⁻) ions remain near the cathode, making an alkaline solution of sodium hydroxide that turns the indicator purple.

Water of crystallization

Some solids take up water, forming crystalline structures. This is called water of crystallization. Hydrated samples of a solid (which contain the maximum amount of water) can be obtained by partially evaporating a solution. The water of crystallization in these hydrated crystals can be removed by heating or using a dehydrating agent such as sulfuric acid, changing them to an ANHYDROUS form.

Demonstration 1: heating hydrated sodium carbonate crystals

To show that a hydrated solid contains water, some hydrated crystals of translucent sodium carbonate decahydrate are heated ($Na_2CO_3 \bullet 10H_2O$) (①). Within a few seconds the solid begins to melt, then boil, and steam is given off (②). The presence of water from this change can be tested because it turns blue cobalt(II) chloride pink. The white powder that remains when the steam stops being evolved is anhydrous sodium carbonate (Na_2CO_3).

Also, if the hydrated crystals are exposed to air (③), they dehydrate, turning to a white anhydrous powder – they are said to EFFLORESCE (④) (see also page 20).

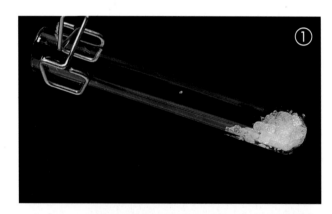

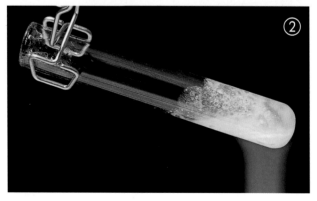

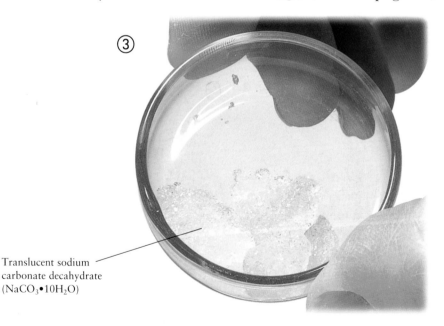

Translucent sodium carbonate decahydrate ($NaCO_3 \bullet 10H_2O$)

Anhydrous sodium carbonate ($NaCO_3$)

Demonstration 2: dehydration of hydrated copper(II) sulfate using concentrated sulfuric acid

A disc of blue hydrated copper(II) sulfate crystals ($CuSO_4 \bullet 5H_2O$, copper(II) sulfate pentahydrate) is prepared and placed in a Petri dish. Some concentrated sulfuric acid is dripped onto a part of the sample (⑤) and allowed to stand for two hours.

Concentrated sulfuric acid has a strong affinity for water (see also page 28) and dehydrates the blue hydrated copper(II) sulfate to form white anhydrous copper(II) sulfate ($CuSO_4$) (⑥).

Remarks

Many of the anhydrous forms of compounds that contain water of crystallization readily absorb moisture to reassume their hydrated condition. Some will change color at the same time. Copper(II) sulfate changes from white to blue, and cobalt(II) chloride ($CoCl_2$) from blue to pink, as water is absorbed. Because of this visible change in color, they can be used to test for, or even remove, moisture in a laboratory experiment (see pages 26, 27, and 30).

Dark blue hydrated copper(II) sulfate crystals, ($CuSO_4 \bullet 5H_2O$)

Some concentrated sulfuric acid is added using a pipette.

Light blue to white anhydrous copper(II) sulfate ($CuSO_4$)

Water as a reactant

Water is, to a very slight extent, ionized; that is, some of the water molecules break down into hydrogen ions and hydroxide ions.

Water ⇨ hydrogen ions + hydroxide ions
$H_2O(l) ⇨ H^+(aq) + OH^-(aq)$

In some cases the reaction with water is violently EXOTHERMIC, as is the case when water reacts with calcium oxide.

Demonstration: reaction of water with calcium oxide

In this demonstration some small blocks of calcium oxide (CaO, which contains calcium ions and oxide ions) are placed in a beaker, and some drops of water are added from a pipette (①).

During the reaction the blocks swell and crack. At the same time, they get very hot, and some of the water is driven off as steam (②). Within a few minutes the hard calcium oxide has been changed into a soft powder of calcium hydroxide (③). The overall reaction is:

Calcium oxide + water ⇨ calcium hydroxide
$CaO(s) + H_2O(l) ⇨ Ca(OH)_2(s)$

After the reaction with water the resultant calcium hydroxide contains calcium ions (which have taken no part in the reaction and so are SPECTATOR IONS) and hydroxide ions. Therefore the real reaction is:

Oxide ions from the calcium oxide + water ⇨ hydroxide ions
$O^{2-}(s) + H_2O(l) ⇨ 2OH^-(s)$

That is, the water molecules have been completely absorbed into the calcium hydroxide.

Water as a catalyst

A catalyst is a substance that increases the rate of a chemical reaction while itself remaining unchanged at the end of the reaction. The name catalyst comes from the Greek word "katalysis," meaning to break up.

Catalysts are effective in very small quantities. The exact way in which a catalyst works is often not understood, although it is thought that the catalyst may form a temporary complex with the reacting materials and thereby reduce the amount of energy needed for the reaction.

In many reactions water is an unsuspected catalyst. Reactions attempted in superdry apparatus often do not work! Normal glassware is covered in a thin, invisible layer of moisture at normal temperature.

In some reactions water is obviously a catalyst because the reactions do not happen until a drop of water is added. Then a violent reaction occurs between the other reactants.

Demonstration: reacting iodine and aluminum using a water catalyst

Some dry aluminum powder is placed on a heat-resistant gauze disc, and iodine crystals mixed with it (①). No change occurs, and no reaction takes place. However, when distilled water is dripped onto the mixture (②), a reaction immediately occurs that releases dense purple iodine fumes (③ & ④). In this case the water acts as a catalyst. (Dripping water onto iodine crystals does not produce any fumes.)

Because iodine is poisonous, this demonstration has to be done in a fume chamber. Also, because friction might well also cause a reaction, the mixing has to be done gently and with care.

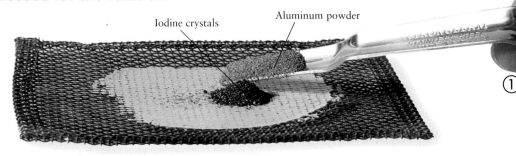

Iodine crystals

Aluminum powder

①

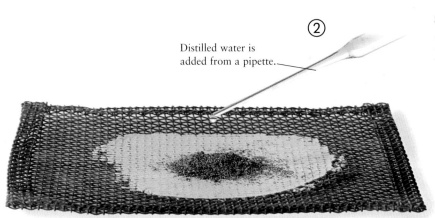

②

Distilled water is added from a pipette.

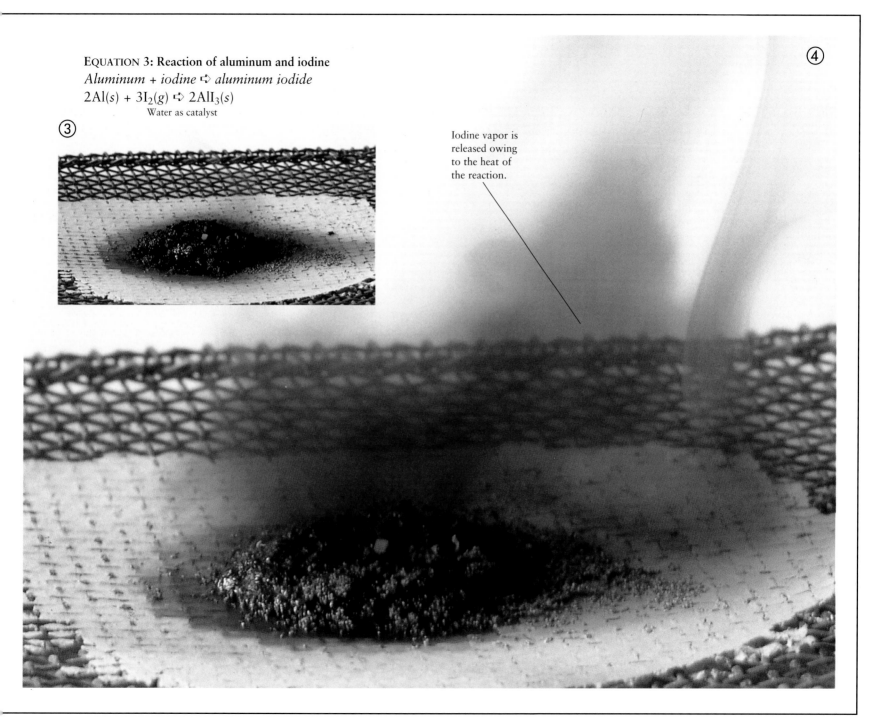

EQUATION 3: Reaction of aluminum and iodine

Aluminum + iodine ⇨ aluminum iodide

$2Al(s) + 3I_2(g) ⇨ 2AlI_3(s)$

Water as catalyst

③

Iodine vapor is released owing to the heat of the reaction.

Water reacting with both acids and bases

Water will react with both acids and bases. Thus the most soluble gases not only dissolve in water but react with it to produce either acidic or alkaline solutions.

Demonstration: reaction of ammonia and water

The extreme solubility of ammonia gas in water, and its alkaline reaction with water, makes the fountain experiment a suitable demonstration of how water produces both hydrogen (H^+) and hydroxide (OH^-) ions.

The apparatus consists of a pneumatic trough filled with water and a large, long-necked flask. The flask is first filled with ammonia gas. It is then clamped with its neck downward over the pneumatic trough. A long, thin, flexible tube is led from the stopper in the flask to the water in the trough. A few drops of the chemical indicator phenolphthalein are now added to the water. The indicator is colorless because the water has a pH of around 7 – is neutral (①).

Ether liquid is poured onto the flask, causing the temperature of the ammonia to drop. The ammonia therefore contracts, and the pressure inside the flask is reduced. As a result, atmospheric pressure is now able to push water from the pneumatic trough up the thin tube and into the flask (②).

As soon as the first drops of water come into contact with the ammonia gas, the ammonia goes into solution, and there is a further rapid drop of pressure in the flask. Atmospheric pressure then causes the

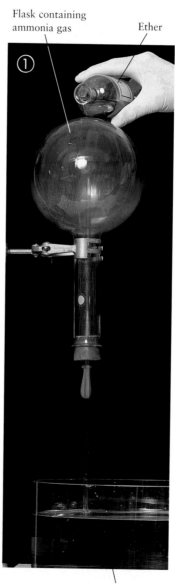

Flask containing ammonia gas

Ether

①

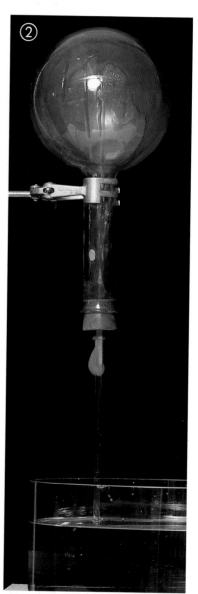

②

Water containing phenolphthalein indicator is colorless when neutral.

Fountain of water immediately turns pink due to the alkaline ammonia.

③

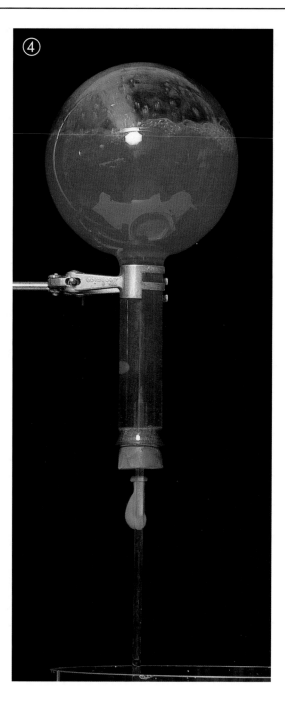

④

water to spurt into the flask (③), producing a fountain. The flask soon fills with bright pink water, as the ammonia turns the water alkaline and thus makes the indicator turn pink (④).

Remarks

By definition, an ACID is a substance that provides hydrogen ions. The hydrogen ions come from the water, which is therefore an acid in this reaction.

When water produces a hydrogen ion, it also produces a hydroxide ion. This is what causes the ALKALINE reaction shown by the indicator.

Ammonia + water ⇨ ammonium ions + hydroxide ions
$NH_3(g) + H_2O(l) ⇨ NH_4^+(aq) + OH^-(aq)$
This can be written as:
$NH_3(g) + H^+(aq) ⇨ NH_4^+(aq)$.

When you test for ammonia using an indicator, it is the hydroxide ions from the water that are causing the alkaline reaction, not the ammonia itself (hence the need to use <u>damp</u> pH paper if the indicator paper is used for the test).

Water produces acidic properties

Any substance that has acidic properties will ionize in water. One test for acidic properties is therefore to test for the presence of ions in solution. Further tests are reaction with a metal such as magnesium and reaction with a carbonate such as anhydrous sodium carbonate.

Demonstration 1: a solution of hydrogen chloride gas in methylbenzene is not acidic

In this demonstration hydrogen chloride gas is prepared in a conical flask by reacting concentrated sulfuric acid and sodium chloride (①). The gas produced is passed through a delivery tube and some rubber tubing to a funnel. The funnel is immersed in some dry (no water) liquid methylbenzene in a beaker. A funnel allows the gas to spread out over a large surface area of the liquid and so maximizes the opportunities for the gas to dissolve.

Hydrogen chloride gas contains no ions. If it is dissolved in dry methylbenzene, the result is hydrogen chloride molecules mixed in with methylbenzene molecules. There are no hydrogen ions and therefore no acidity to the solution.

The solution of hydrogen chloride and methylbenzene can now be tested for an acid reaction. Two test tubes are made up with the colorless solution. A piece of magnesium ribbon is placed in one (②), and anhydrous sodium carbonate is placed in the other (③).

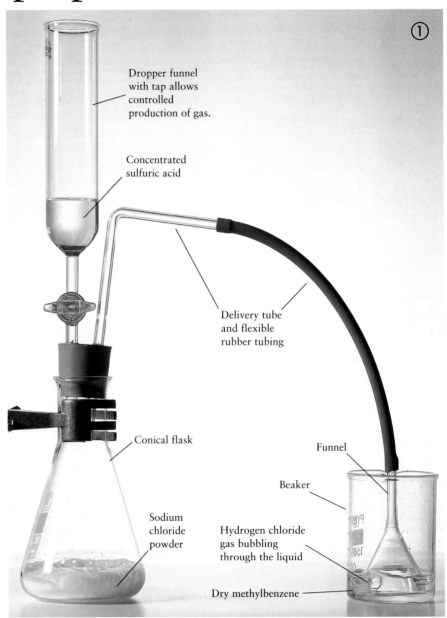

①

Dropper funnel with tap allows controlled production of gas.

Concentrated sulfuric acid

Delivery tube and flexible rubber tubing

Conical flask

Funnel

Beaker

Sodium chloride powder

Hydrogen chloride gas bubbling through the liquid

Dry methylbenzene

These two test tubes contain dry methylbenzene solution of hydrogen chloride.

These two test tubes contain an aqueous solution of hydrogen chloride.

Magnesium ribbon does not react and sinks.

Anhydrous sodium carbonate does not react.

Magnesium ribbon reacts, releasing bubbles of hydrogen gas that lift the metal to the surface.

Anhydrous sodium carbonate reacts, releasing bubbles of carbon dioxide.

No reaction occurs in either tube, showing that hydrogen chloride gas cannot behave as an acid in a solution without water.

Demonstration 2: a solution of hydrogen chloride in water is acidic

The demonstration is repeated, but this time the hydrogen chloride gas is bubbled through distilled water as the solution in the beaker. The result is an aqueous solution of hydrogen chloride (hydrochloric acid).

Some of the aqueous solution is poured into two test tubes and once again tested for an acid reaction. A piece of magnesium ribbon is placed in one (④), and some anhydrous sodium carbonate is placed in the other (⑤). Vigorous reactions occur in both test tubes. At the end of these reactions the sodium carbonate and the magnesium ribbon have "dissolved" entirely, showing that there was an excess of acid in the tubes, while the first two tubes remain with unreacted reagents in them. (Addition of water to the tubes containing the methylbenzene solution causes reactions as in tubes ④ and ⑤.)

The reaction of water with metals

The most reactive metals (those in Groups 1 and 2 of the Periodic Table) react with water, releasing hydrogen and yielding an alkaline metal hydroxide. One way of looking at the reaction of water with these metals is to consider that the hydrogen ion of the water is actually reacting with the metal, that is, the water is behaving as an acid.

The hydroxides produced by Group 1 metals (such as sodium and potassium) are soluble (they produce strong BASES), while the hydroxides produced by Group 2 metals (such as calcium and barium) are less soluble (although they are also strong bases).

Demonstration 1: reaction of sodium with water

If a piece of sodium is dropped into water in a shallow beaker to which phenolphthalein indicator has been added (①), the pellet immediately begins to react. Hydrogen is released in the reaction, buoying up and propelling the pellet along the surface, forming a fizzing trail (②).

The reaction also produces sodium hydroxide, which is strongly alkaline and causes the phenolphthalein indicator to turn pink (② & ③). The sodium hydroxide is soluble, and so the solution in the beaker remains clear throughout the reaction, and no solid precipitate is seen.

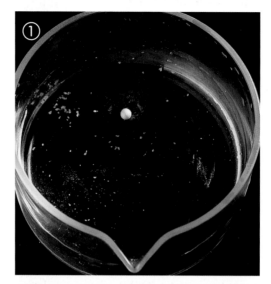
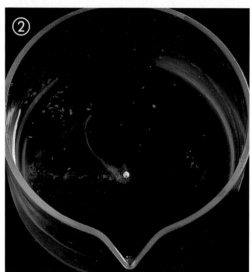
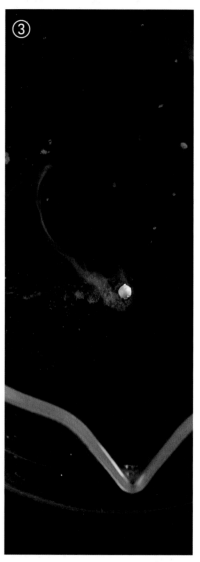

EQUATION: Reaction of sodium metal with water
Sodium + water ⇨ sodium hydroxide + hydrogen
$2Na(s) + 2H_2O(l) ⇨ 2NaOH(aq) + H_2(g)$

46

The heat released from the reaction makes the metal form a rolling molten ball and turns some of the water to steam. The pellet of sodium used in this demonstration had reacted completely within 20 seconds.

Demonstration 2: reaction of calcium with water

When a small pellet of calcium is placed in a shallow beaker of water (without indicator solution), it sinks to the bottom. At this stage an upturned test tube that has been filled with water is placed over the pellet.

A reaction between the calcium and the water begins. Hydrogen is released (④) in sufficient quantity for bubbles to buoy up the calcium pellet and carry it to the surface (⑤). Here the hydrogen bubbles burst, and the pellet begins to sink until enough new bubbles have formed to raise the pellet to the surface again (⑥). In this way the calcium pellet bobs up and down in the test tube.

The hydrogen displaces the water from the test tube, and the reaction continues for approximately a minute until all the metal has reacted.

The reaction of the calcium with the water quickly saturates the water in the test tube with calcium hydroxide (also known as limewater). More calcium hydroxide is now insoluble and forms tiny granular particles (precipitate) that remain suspended in the water, turning the water cloudy (⑦).

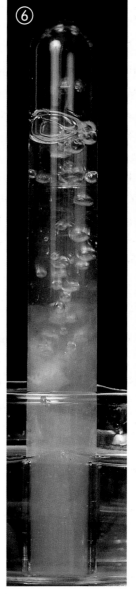

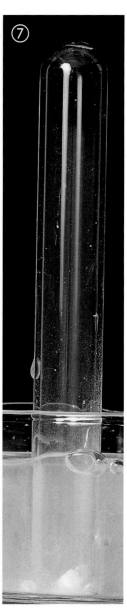

EQUATION: Reaction of calcium metal with water

Calcium + water ⇨ *hydrogen gas + calcium hydroxide*

$Ca(s) + 2H_2O(l) ⇨ H_2(g) + Ca(OH)_2(aq)$

Solubility in water

Any solution contains a (liquid) SOLVENT and a (solid or gas or liquid) SOLUTE. When as much solute is dissolved or contained in a solvent as possible at a particular temperature, the solution is said to be saturated. This demonstration shows how to find out the amount of solute required to produce a SATURATED SOLUTION in a solvent at room temperature. A variety of solutes are compared for their solubility in a solvent, water.

Demonstration: finding the solubility of a solute

A saturated solution of the solute under test must first be prepared. To do this, the solid solute is added to a beaker about half filled with the solvent (①). The solvent used here is distilled water.

Small amounts of the solute are added gradually to the water and stirred using a stirring thermometer. When no more solute will dissolve, the solution is saturated (②). The reading on the thermometer is taken.

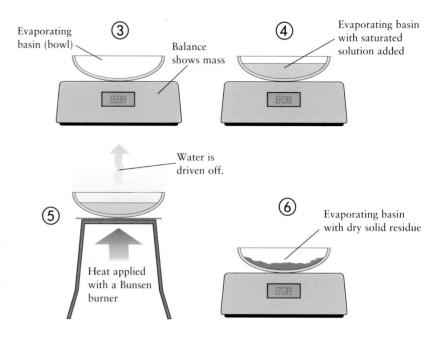

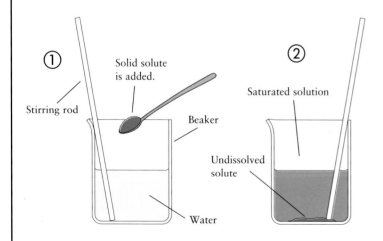

The solution produced by dissolving any solute in water is described as an aqueous solution. It is important to note that the use of distilled water as opposed to tap water is important because tap water already contains dissolved solids (solutes).

Next, the mass of the solute dissolved in a given volume of solvent to make the saturated solution must be measured. An evaporating basin is weighed (③). Some of the saturated solution is poured into it (④), and the evaporating basin and its contents are then reweighed. The evaporating basin and solution are then gently heated using a Bunsen flame (⑤) until the water has evaporated completely and only dry solid remains (⑥). After allowing the basin to cool, the basin and this residue are then weighed again.

Calculation

Using the measurements, the solubility of the solute in water can be calculated as follows:

Mass of evaporating basin = a grams
Mass of evaporating basin and solution = b grams
The mass of the evaporated solute and basin = c grams
Therefore the mass of solute is $c - a = d$ grams,
and the mass of water evaporated is $b - c = e$ grams.
Because 1 cm^3 of distilled water has a mass of 1 gram, then d grams of solute were dissolved in e cm^3 of water.
This result can now be multiplied to show the mass of solute that will dissolve in 100 cm^3 to make a saturated solution – the solubility – at this temperature.

Results

The masses of various solutes dissolved in 100 cm^3 of water at 25°C using this method are shown in the photograph (⑥). It is clear that some substances, such as sodium thiosulfate, are extremely soluble in water, while others, such as calcium hydroxide, are not.

It is important to realize that the amount of solute that can be held depends on the temperature of the solution. This is the reason why all of the solubilities shown in this demonstration were performed at a standard 25°C. The variation in solubility with temperature is shown in the demonstration on page 50.

100 cm^3 of distilled water at 25°C. The masses of each of the solids shown here will dissolve in this volume of water to make a saturated solution.

Sodium thiosulfate ($Na_2S_2O_3$), 302.0 g

Iron(III) chloride ($FeCl_2$), 196.0 g

Potassium permanganate (potassium manganate(VII), $KMnO_4$), 32.0 g

Potassium perchlorate (potassium chlorate(VI), $KClO_4$), 6.5 g

Potassium dichromate(VI) ($K_2Cr_2O_7$), 37.0 g

Calcium hydroxide ($Ca(OH)_2$), 0.1 g

Solubility varies with temperature

In general, the solubility of a substance increases with increasing temperature, as this demonstration shows.

Demonstration: solubility of potassium chlorate

The apparatus consists of a boiling tube, a burette and a stirring thermometer, and a laboratory balance. Because this is a quantitative demonstration, weights and volumes have to be measured and recorded for each step.

To investigate changes in solubility, 5 g of potassium chlorate (potassium chlorate(V), $KClO_3$) (①) is weighed out into a boiling tube (② & ③). 10 cm^3 of distilled water are added from a burette (④ & ⑤), and the mixture heated over a Bunsen flame while being stirred with a stirring thermometer (⑥, see page 52). The objective of heating is to raise the temperature of the water in the tube enough to allow all of the potassium chlorate to dissolve.

When all of the solid has dissolved to make a colorless solution, the boiling tube is allowed to cool, but the stirring is continued. The temperature of the solution is taken when the first crystals appear (⑦), which for this volume of water was 98°C. At this stage almost all of the potassium chlorate remains dissolved, and the solution has just become saturated. Therefore, at this temperature 10 cm^3 of water dissolves 5 g of potassium chlorate. This is the maximum solubility at this temperature.

Another 5 cm^3 of water are added, the boiling tube is reheated until all of the potassium chlorate has dissolved, and then it is allowed to cool. As before,

① Crystals of potassium chlorate

② Scales are set to zero with the test tube.

③ The potassium chlorate is now weighed.

④ Burette filled with water

⑤

the temperature when the first crystals appear is recorded. This time, when the first crystals appear, the temperature is found to be lower than before. This is the solubility with a slightly higher dilution.

The demonstration is continued for additional quantities of water (⑧, see page 53) so that a table of data can be tabulated (⑨), and from this a graph of the various levels of solubility against temperature can be drawn (⑩).

Solubility can be expressed as the mass (in grams) of a solute per 100 grams of solvent. So, 5 g of potassium chlorate dissolving in 10 cm^3 of water (1 cm^3 of water is equal to 1 gm, so 10 cm^3 is equal to 10 g) corresponds to 50 g in 100 g or a solubility of 50.

Remarks

Notice that the curve is obtained by progressively diluting a solution. This is a better use of the reactant than making a range of samples each with the same amount of water but a different amount of reactant in. The curved shape of the graph shows that although solubility does increase with temperature, it is not a linear (straight line) relationship, and in fact, solubility increases much faster than temperature.

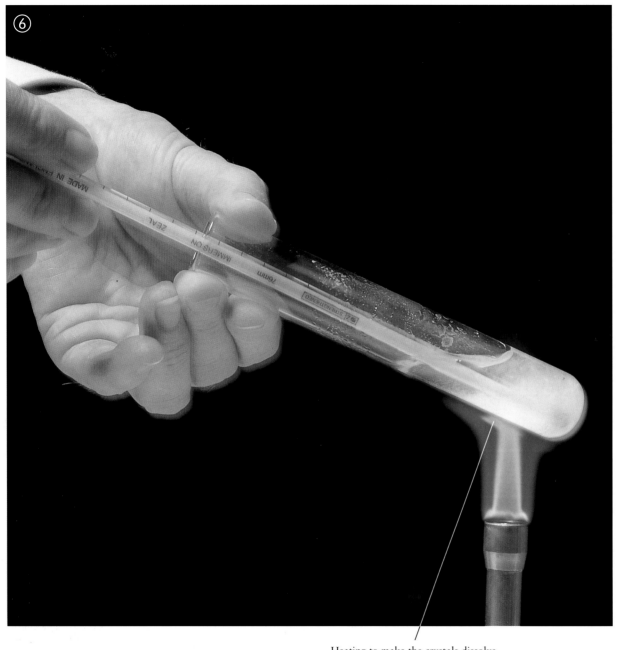

Heating to make the crystals dissolve

⑧

A total of 20 cm³ of water has been added.

NOTE: A considerable amount of solid crystallizes if the solution in 15 cm³ of water is allowed to cool to near room temperature.

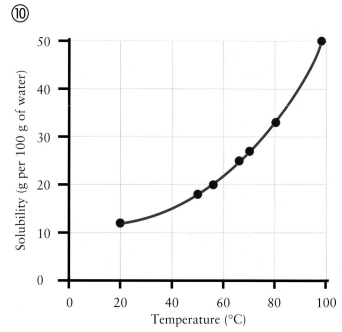

⑨ TABLE Solubility of potassium chlorate	
Solubility (g per 100 g of water)	Temperature (°C)
50	98
33	80
27	70
25	66
20	56
18	50
12	20

⑩

Water as an oxidizing agent

Water often acts as an oxidizing agent. For example, water can oxidize white-hot carbon to carbon monoxide while the water itself is reduced to hydrogen gas, as shown in this demonstration.

Demonstration: oxidizing carbon with steam to produce water gas

Carbon and water only react at high temperatures. So for this demonstration water is used in the form of steam, and carbon has to be heated in a laboratory furnace until it is white-hot.

Carbon, in the form of charcoal chunks, is placed in a heat-resistant silica tube inside the furnace (①). A supply of steam is provided by heating a metal

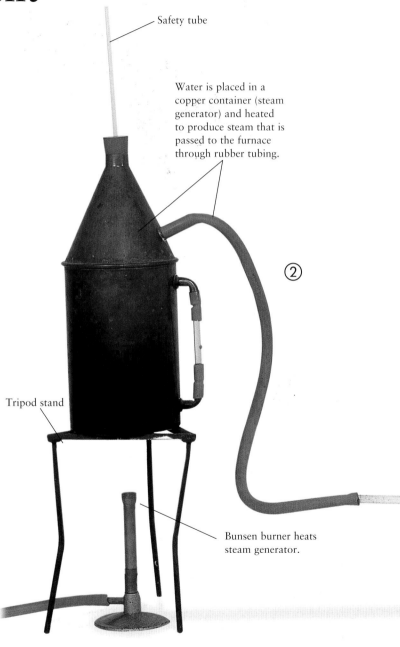

Safety tube

Water is placed in a copper container (steam generator) and heated to produce steam that is passed to the furnace through rubber tubing.

②

Tripod stand

Bunsen burner heats steam generator.

①

Charcoal (carbon) is placed in the silica tube.

Furnace consisting of a silica tube heated by gas jets. Heat is conserved by surrounding the apparatus with a ceramic liner.

container partly filled with water, using a Bunsen flame (②). The steam generator and the silica tube are connected with flexible tubing.

In the furnace the steam oxidizes the carbon to carbon monoxide and is itself reduced to hydrogen. The gases are collected in a gas jar over water.

The reaction of steam and carbon is an example of a significantly ENDOTHERMIC reaction, that is, the reaction takes in heat, which is why heat energy in the form of a gas flame has to be applied continually (③).

Water gas is formed, which is a one-to-one (by volume) mixture of hydrogen and carbon monoxide.

Remarks

Oxidation and reduction are complementary processes, so this demonstration can also be viewed as the reduction of steam using carbon.

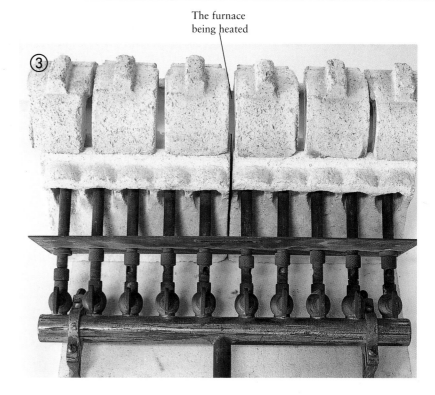

③ The furnace being heated

EQUATION: Oxidation of white-hot carbon using steam
Water + carbon ⇨ *carbon monoxide + hydrogen*
$H_2O(g) + C(s) ⇨ CO(g) + H_2(g)$

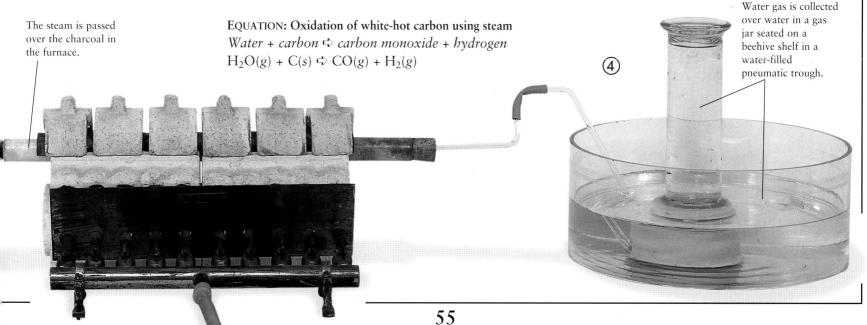

The steam is passed over the charcoal in the furnace.

④ Water gas is collected over water in a gas jar seated on a beehive shelf in a water-filled pneumatic trough.

Water as a reducing agent

Whether a substance behaves as an oxidizing agent or a reducing agent depends on the relative oxidizing or reducing strength of the substance it is reacting with. Chlorine, for example, is a very strong oxidizing agent, and in its presence water behaves as a reducing agent, as this demonstration shows.

Chlorine is very poisonous, and so these demonstrations are done in a fume chamber.

Demonstration: bleaching pH paper with chlorine

Chlorine is a yellowish-green acidic gas that is a powerful oxidizing agent and a bleach.

In this demonstration chlorine has been generated by reacting dilute hydrochloric acid with sodium chlorate(I).

When damp green pH paper (①) is exposed to the chlorine gas, at first it turns red (②). The change in color of the organic compounds that make up the indicator shows that the solution is acidic. However, the indicator is then quickly bleached (③). The bleaching occurs because the chlorine oxidizes the water on the paper, liberating oxygen. It is actually the liberated oxygen that then oxidizes the colored organic compound, thus making it colorless.

Remarks

In the presence of sunlight water may also reduce chlorine gas to hydrogen chloride, releasing oxygen gas (④).

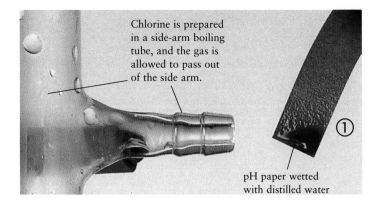

Chlorine is prepared in a side-arm boiling tube, and the gas is allowed to pass out of the side arm.

pH paper wetted with distilled water

①

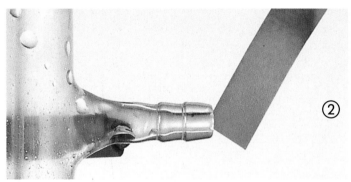

②

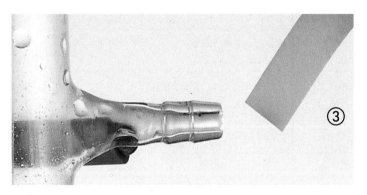

③

④ EQUATION: Reducing chlorine gas with water in sunlight
Chlorine + water ⇨ hydrochloric acid + oxygen
$2Cl_2(g) + 2H_2O(l) \Rightarrow 4HCl(aq) + O_2(g)$
Ultraviolet light

Water hardness

There are many compounds dissolved in water, but in water supplies calcium and magnesium compounds are among the most common. If water supplies contain more than 120 milligrams of these compounds in each liter of water, the water is described as "hard" water.

In general, if water does not lather easily using soap, the water is hard. The source of most hardness in water is limestone, so if water supplies are collected from limestone groundwater or if water is taken from rivers that flow over limestone rocks, then water supplies will be hard.

One of the most important results of heating hard water is the production of limescale. This is a combination of the precipitates of calcium and magnesium carbonates. Carbonates are readily precipitated when hard water is heated because the stability of the bicarbonates decreases with temperature. This is why limescale is found on the heating element of a coffee jug or electric kettle.

Temporary and permanent hardness

Water hardness can be either temporary or permanent. Water containing soluble calcium hydrogen carbonate (calcium bicarbonate) is temporarily hard because calcium hydrogen carbonates can be removed by boiling (the carbonate precipitates). Water is permanently hard if it contains calcium or magnesium salts other than the hydrogen carbonates, since these cannot be removed by boiling. It does not produce scale in kettles, but it does make it difficult to obtain a lather with soap.

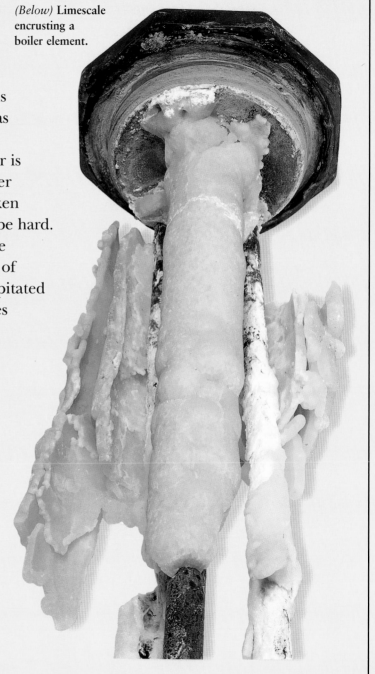

(Below) Limescale encrusting a boiler element.

EQUATION: Precipitating limescale

Calcium hydrogen carbonate ⇨ *carbon dioxide + water + calcium carbonate*

$$Ca(HCO_3)_2(aq) \Rightarrow CO_2(g) + H_2O(l) + CaCO_3(s)$$
Precipitate

Demonstration: determination of the ratio of permanent to temporary water hardness

It is possible to estimate the degree of permanent hardness in water using the technique of TITRATION and a soap solution.

Since this demonstration is quantitative, recordings are required at each stage.

The apparatus consists of a conical flask and a burette. A measured amount of tap water (in this demonstration it was 20cm³) is placed in a conical flask (①). Soap solution (soap dissolved in distilled water) is then added from a burette placed over the flask (②).

The flask is agitated constantly until the first signs of a froth (lather) appear (③). At this point the soap solution has counteracted the effect of both temporary and permanent hardness. The volume of soap solution added is then recorded.

The demonstration is repeated using identical quantities of the same supply of tap water that has been:

(i) boiled (boiling the tap water removes temporary hardness)

(ii) distilled (distilled water is the steam collected from boiling the tap water and contains neither temporary nor permanent hardness).

Calculation

The volume of soap solution needed to produce a
    lather in tap water = a cm³

The volume of soap solution needed to produce a
    lather in boiled tap water = b cm³

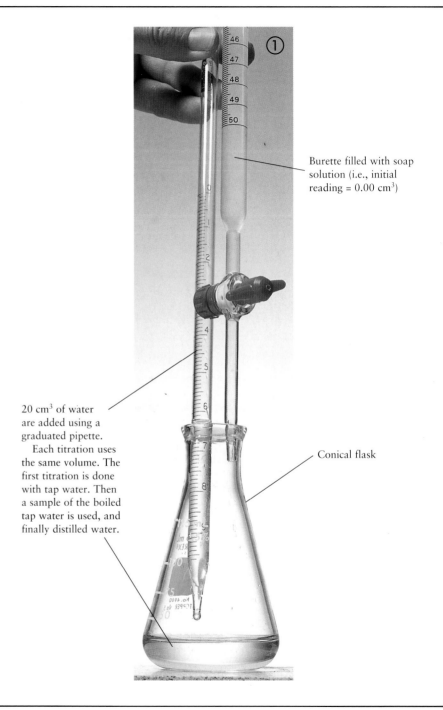

Burette filled with soap solution (i.e., initial reading = 0.00 cm³)

20 cm³ of water are added using a graduated pipette.
    Each titration uses the same volume. The first titration is done with tap water. Then a sample of the boiled tap water is used, and finally distilled water.

Conical flask

② ③

Once the first lather occurs, a second reading is taken from the burette so that the amount of soap solution used can be calculated.

Soap solution is added. The tap water is turned cloudy, but at this stage no lather can be seen on the surface.

The volume of soap solution needed to produce a lather in distilled water = c cm^3

The ratio of permanent to temporary hardness is:

$$\frac{b - c}{a - b} = \frac{\text{permanent hardness}}{\text{temporary hardness}}$$

Remarks

The amount of soap solution required to produce a froth on the distilled water is very small – in this demonstration it was 1 cm^3 of soap solution, whereas with boiled tap water the amount of soap solution used was 15 cm^3, and with ordinary tap water 30 cm^3. This gives a ratio of 1.07, which indicates hard water.

These values are, of course, not fixed but depend on the nature of the water supply and the concentration of the soap solution. But they give an indication of the differences to be expected.

The method is of limited accuracy because of the need to make a subjective decision about when the froth is or is not present.

It is a mistake to titrate the distilled water sample first because a good "head" of froth is easy to obtain that cannot then be matched by the tap water, whereas the scummy froth obtained in the tap water titration can always be matched in the distilled water titration.

Air-water interaction

Many chemical reactions in the environment involve the interaction of air and water. Heating a bowl of water and watching the bubbles appear, for example, shows that at least some of the gases in the air readily dissolve in water and can be set free by heating.

Gases also dissolve in water droplets in the air. For example, carbon dioxide from the air interacts with water droplets to produce carbonic acid. This is the acid that is primarily responsible for the sculpting of limestone landscapes worldwide.

Similarly, pollutant gases such as nitrogen dioxide and sulfur dioxide react with air and droplets near industrial areas and over cities to produce nitric and sulfuric acids, and these fall as ACID RAIN.

Demonstration 1: the interaction of carbon dioxide and water

In this demonstration a continuous flow of carbon dioxide gas is required. This is prepared most easily by using Kipp's apparatus (①). The delivery tube from the Kipp's apparatus is taken to a gas jar that contains tap water and a few drops of Universal Indicator, so that we can readily see the changes taking place (②).

At the start of the demonstration, the solution is green-blue because the tap water used is alkaline, but

① Kipp's apparatus

The carbon dioxide gas is led off through a delivery tube.

Hydrochloric acid is reacted with calcium carbonate chips to produce carbon dioxide gas.

②

as carbon dioxide bubbles through, the color changes quickly to a strong green (③), then to a yellowy-green (④), then a yellow (⑤), and finally pink (⑥), indicating that it is a weak acid.

EQUATION: Reaction of carbon dioxide and water
Carbon dioxide + water ⇨ carbonic acid
$CO_2(g) + H_2O(l) ⇨ H_2CO_3(aq)$

③ ④ ⑤ ⑥

Bubbles of carbon dioxide

Demonstration 2: oxygen dissolves in water (oxygenation of water)

Although it is possible to see the gases dissolved in water being released prior to boiling, this does not indicate which gases are dissolved. This demonstration uses a reaction that is sensitive to oxygen and clearly visible to show that oxygen is one of the gases dissolved in the water.

Concentrated ammonia solution is added to a test tube containing white copper(I) chloride using a pipette ((7)). This produces a colorless solution of copper(I) ammine. However, in the presence of oxygen copper(I) ammine is rapidly oxidized to copper(II) ammine, which is a deep indigo-blue color ((8)).

The way to see that this effect is produced by oxygen from the air is to let the test tube containing the copper(I) ammine stand. Within a few moments a very deep blue layer begins to form on the surface in the part of the solution that can be reached by the air.

The first signs of a color change occur in the meniscus, where the liquid meets the air. In fact, by watching the changing color of the liquid, it is possible to investigate the rate at which oxygen dissolves in still water. Over some minutes air dissolves in the solution to about one and a half centimeters depth, and thus the blue color gradually extends into the solution.

If the blue-colored part of the liquid is pipetted off so that all the solution is colorless again, the surface part of the solution rapidly changes to a blue color as oxidation recurs at the MENISCUS ((9) & (10)).

Finally, if the tube is shaken, oxygen can dissolve throughout the liquid, and the contents of the tube turn completely blue ((11)).

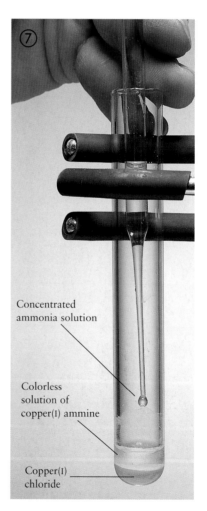

(7)

Concentrated ammonia solution

Colorless solution of copper(I) ammine

Copper(I) chloride

(8)

Deep indigo-blue copper(II) ammine

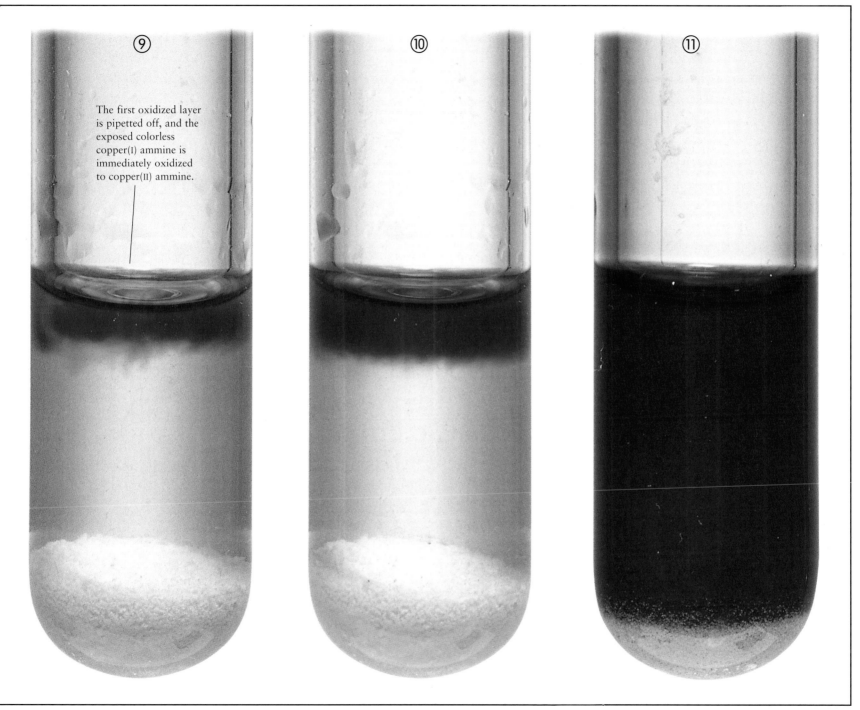

The first oxidized layer
is pipetted off, and the
exposed colorless
copper(I) ammine is
immediately oxidized
to copper(II) ammine.

Corrosion of metals in air and water

Most metals react with air and water. In the process the metal is oxidized and CORRODED (see page 46). The most economically important form of corrosion is the rusting of iron.

The water, and air dissolved in it, acts as an electrolyte in tiny electrochemical reactions that occur on the irregular surface of the bare iron. Once oxidized, the iron is a much weaker material. Rust is an orange color and flaky.

Iron nail remains uncorroded.

Water containing phenolphthalein indicator

Over about a week the iron nail is corroded.

Magnesium strip is corroding within a few minutes.

Tin strip remains uncorroded.

Demonstration 1: relative reactivity of metals in aerated water

The apparatus consists of two small bottles filled with distilled water. One container has an iron nail with a small piece of magnesium wrapped around it (①); the other has a nail with a small piece of tin wrapped around it (②). A few drops of colorless phenolphthalein indicator are added to the water. Phenolphthalein turns pink where an electrochemical reaction occurs.

The REACTIVITY of magnesium relative to iron and tin is demonstrated here. In the bottle on the left a reaction takes place at the magnesium strip, causing the formation of magnesium hydroxide, an alkaline substance that makes the indicator turn purple. The iron nail is not corroded because magnesium is more reactive than iron.

By contrast, in the right-hand bottle the tin has not reacted, and the iron nail has corroded (rusted). This is because iron is more reactive than tin.

Remarks

The greater reactivity of magnesium in aerated water compared with iron can be used to advantage to reduce the rate of corrosion of iron or steel used in construction or manufacturing. Notice that this demonstration also explains why, when a tin-plated container is scratched, it is not protected by the tin, but, in fact, the iron is subjected to greater corrosion by the presence of the tin. This is one reason why tin plating is not as widely used now as in the past.

Demonstration 2: determining the percentage of oxygen in the air by rusting

This demonstration is a parallel to that shown on page 12. In this case some iron filings are poured into the long, graduated, tube, which is then almost filled with water and upturned into a gas jar nearly full of water (③).

As the tube is righted, the iron filings are spread all the way down the tube (④), and they will rust and use up the oxygen inside the tube. Because they have a large surface area, rusting occurs quite quickly.

As a result of rapid rusting (⑤) the demonstration works more quickly, and it will come close to its final volume in 2 to 3 days and reach its final volume in 2 to 3 weeks rather than the 2 to 3 months required for phosphorus.

The rusting iron uses up about a fifth of the original volume of air in the graduated tube. This is the approximate proportion of oxygen in the air.

Remarks

Contrast this demonstration with the phosphorus used in the demonstration on page 12, where the oxidizing phosphorus was in a single lump, and where the phosphorus did not react with the water. In the case of iron rusting will not occur in the absence of water.

Graduated tube, dampened inside with water, half filled with air and iron filings distributed along its length.

Rusted iron filings

Gas jar filled with water

EQUATION: Overall reaction for the rusting of iron
Iron + water + oxygen ⇨ iron(III) oxide + water
$4Fe(s) + H_2O(l) + 3O_2(g) ⇨ 2Fe_2O_3(s) + H_2O(l)$
Rust

MASTER GLOSSARY

absolute zero: the lowest possible temperature (−273.15°C).

absorption: the process by which a substance is soaked up. *See:* adsorption.

acid: a substance that can give a proton to another substance. Acids are compounds containing hydrogen that can attack and dissolve many substances. Acids are described as weak or strong, dilute or concentrated, mineral or organic. *Example:* hydrochloric acid (HCl). An acid in water can react with a base to form a salt and water.

acidic solution: a solution with a pH lower than 7. *See:* pH.

acidity: a general term for the strength of an acid in a solution.

acid radical: the negative ion left behind when an acid loses a hydrogen ion. *Example:* Cl⁻ in hydrochloric acid (HCl).

acid salt: An ACID SALT contains at least one hydrogen ion and can behave as an acid in chemical reactions. Acid salts are produced under conditions that do not allow complete neutralization of the acid. For example, sulfuric acid may react with a sodium compound to produce a normal sodium salt, sodium sulfate (Na_2SO_4), or it may retain some of the hydrogen, in which case it becomes the salt sodium hydrogen sulfate ($NaHSO_4$).

actinide series or actinide metals: a series of 15 similar radioactive elements between actinium and lawrencium. They are transition metals.

activated charcoal: a form of carbon made of tiny crystals of graphite that is made by heating organic matter in the absence of air. It is then further processed to increase its pore space and therefore its surface area. Its surface area is about 2000 m^2/g. Activated charcoal readily adsorbs many gases, and it is therefore widely used as a filter, for example, in gas masks.

activation energy: the energy required to make a reaction occur. The greater the activation energy of a reaction, the more its reaction rate depends on temperature. The activation energy of a reaction is useful because, if the rate of reaction is known at one temperature (for example, 100 °C) then the activation energy can be used to calculate the rate of reaction at another temperature (for example, at 400 °C) without actually doing the experiment.

adsorption: the process by which a surface adsorbs a substance. The substances involved are not chemically combined and can be separated. *See:* absorption.

alchemy: the traditional "art" of working with chemicals common in the Middle Ages. One of the main challenges for alchemists was to make gold from lead. Alchemy faded away as scientific chemistry was developed in the 17th century.

alcohol: an organic compound that contains a hydroxyl (OH) group. *Example:* ethanol (CH_3CH_2OH), also known as ethyl alcohol or grain alcohol.

alkali/alkaline: a base in (aqueous) solution. Alkalis react with or neutralize hydrogen ions in acids and have a pH greater than 7.0 because they contain relatively few hydrogen ions. *Example:* aqueous sodium hydroxide (NaOH). *See:* pH.

alkaline cell (or battery): a dry cell in which the electrolyte contains sodium or potassium hydroxide.

alkaline earth metal: a member of Group 2 of the Periodic Table. *Example:* calcium.

alkali metals: a member of Group 1 of the Periodic Table. *Example:* sodium.

alkane: a hydrocarbon with no carbon-to-carbon multiple bonds. *Example:* ethane, C_2H_6.

alkene: a hydrocarbon with at least one carbon-to-carbon double bond. *Example:* ethylene, C_2H_4.

alkyne: a hydrocarbon with at least one carbon-to-carbon triple bond. *Example:* acetylene, C_2H_2.

allotropes: alternative forms of an element that differ in the way the atoms are linked. *Example:* white and red phosphorus.

alloy: a mixture of a metal and various other elements. *Example:* brass is an alloy of copper and zinc.

amalgam: a liquid alloy of mercury with another metal.

amorphous: a solid in which the atoms are not arranged regularly (i.e., "glassy"). Compare crystalline.

amphoteric: a metal that will react with both acids and alkalis. *Example:* aluminum metal.

anhydrous: lacking water; water has been removed, for example by heating. (Opposite of anhydrous is hydrous or hydrated.) *Example:* copper(II) sulfate can be anhydrous ($CuSO_4$) or hydrated ($CuSO_4 \cdot 5H_2O$).

anion: a negatively charged atom or group of atoms. *Examples:* chloride ion (Cl⁻), hydroxide ion (OH⁻).

anode: the electrode at which oxidation occurs; the negative terminal of a battery or the positive electrode of an electrolysis cell.

anodizing: a process that uses the effect of electrolysis to make a surface corrosion-resistant. *Example:* anodized aluminum.

antacid: a common name for any compound that reacts with stomach acid to neutralize it. *Example:* sodium hydrogen carbonate, also known as sodium bicarbonate.

antioxidant: a substance that reacts rapidly with radicals, thereby preventing oxidation of some other substance.

antibumping granules: small glass or ceramic beads designed to promote boiling without the development of large gas bubbles.

approximate relative atomic mass: *See:* relative atomic mass.

aqueous: a solution in which the solvent is water. Usually used as "aqueous solution." *Example:* aqueous solution of sodium hydroxide (NaOH(*aq*)).

aromatic hydrocarbons: compounds of carbon that have the benzene ring as part of their structure. *Examples:* benzene (C_6H_6), naphthalene ($C_{10}H_8$). They are known as aromatic because of their strong pungent smell.

atmospheric pressure: the pressure exerted by the gases in the air. Units of measurement are kilopascals (kPa), atmospheres (atm), millimeters of mercury (mm Hg), and Torr. Standard atmospheric pressure is 100 kPa, 1atm, 760 mm Hg or 760 Torr.

atom: the smallest particle of an element; a nucleus and its surrounding electrons.

atomic mass: the mass of an atom measured in atomic mass units (u). An atomic mass unit equals one twelfth of the atom of carbon-12.

"Atomic mass" is now more generally used than "atomic weight." *Example:* the atomic mass of chlorine is about 35 u. *See:* atomic weight, relative atomic mass.

atomic number: also known as proton number. The number of electrons or the number of protons in an atom. *Example:* the atomic number of gold is 79.

atomic structure: the nucleus and the arrangement of electrons around it.

atomic weight: a common term used to mean the average molar mass of an element (g/mol). This is the mass per mole of atoms. *Example:* the atomic weight of chlorine is about 35 g/mol. *See:* atomic mass, mole.

base: a substance that can accept a proton from another substance. *Example:* aqueous ammonia ($NH_3(aq)$). A base can react with an acid in water to form a salt and water.

basic salt: a salt that contains at least one hydroxide ion. The hydroxide ion can then behave as a base in chemical reactions. *Example:* the reaction of hydrochloric acid (HCl) with the base aluminum hydroxide ($Al(OH)_3$) can form two basic salts, $Al(OH)_2Cl$ and $Al(OH)Cl_2$.

battery: a number of electrochemical cells placed in series.

bauxite: a hydrated impure oxide of aluminum ($Al_2O_3 \cdot xH_2O$, with the amount of water x being variable). It is the main ore used to obtain aluminum metal. The reddish brown color of bauxite is mainly caused by the iron oxide impurities it contains.

beehive shelf: an inverted earthenware bowl with a hole in the upper surface and a slot in the rim. Traditionally the earthenware was brown and looked similar to a beehive, hence its name. A delivery tube passes through the slot, and a gas jar is placed over the hole. This provides a convenient way to collect gas over water in a pneumatic trough.

bell jar: a tall glass jar with an open bottom and a wide, stoppered neck that is used in conjunction with a beehive shelf and a pneumatic trough in some experiments involving gases. The name derives from historic versions of the apparatus, which resembled a bell in shape.

blast furnace: a tall furnace charged with a mixture of iron ore, coke, and limestone and used for the refining of iron metal. The name comes from the strong blast of air introduced during smelting.

bleach: a substance that removes color from stains on materials either by oxidizing or reducing the staining compound. *Example:* sulfur dioxide (SO_2).

block: one of the main divisions of the Periodic Table. Blocks are named for the outermost occupied electron shell of an element. *Example:* the Transition Metals all belong to the d-block.

boiling point: the temperature at which a liquid boils, changing from a liquid to a gas. Boiling points change with atmospheric pressure. *Example:* The boiling point of pure water at standard atmospheric pressure is 100 °C.

boiling tube: A thin glass tube closed at one end and used for chemical tests. The composition and thickness of the glass is such that it cannot sustain very high temperatures and is intended for heating liquids to boiling point. *See:* side-arm boiling tube, test tube.

bond: chemical bonding is either a transfer or sharing of electrons by two or more atoms. There are a number of types of chemical bond, some very strong (such as covalent and ionic bonds), others weak (such as hydrogen bonds). Chemical bonds form because the linked molecule is more stable than the unlinked atoms from which it formed. *Example:* the hydrogen molecule (H_2) is more stable than single atoms of hydrogen, which is why hydrogen gas is always found as molecules of two hydrogen atoms.

Boyle's Law: At constant temperature, and for a given mass of gas, the volume of the gas (V) is inversely proportional to pressure that builds up (P): $P \propto 1/V$.

brine: a solution of salt (sodium chloride, NaCl) in water.

Büchner flask: a thick-walled side-arm flask designed to withstand the changes in pressure that occur when the flask is connected to a suction pump.

Büchner funnel: a special design of plastic or ceramic funnel that has a flat stage on which a filter paper can be placed. It is intended for use under suction with a Büchner funnel.

buffer (solution): a mixture of substances in solution that resists a change in the acidity or alkalinity of the solution when small amounts of an acid or alkali are added.

burette: a long, graduated glass tube with a tap at one end. A burette is used vertically, with the tap lowermost, as a reservoir for a chemical during titration.

burn: a combustion reaction in which a flame is produced. A flame occurs where *gases* combust and release heat and light. At least two gases are therefore required if there is to be a flame. *Example:* methane gas (CH_4) burns in oxygen gas (O_2) to produce carbon dioxide (CO_2) and water (H_2O) and give out heat and light.

calorimeter: an insulated container designed to prevent heat gain or loss with the environment and thus allow changes of temperature within reacting chemicals to be measured accurately. It is named after the old unit of heat, the calorie.

capillary: a very small diameter (glass) tube. Capillary tubing has a small enough diameter to allow surface tension effects to retain water within the tube.

capillary action: the tendency for a liquid to be sucked into small spaces, such as between objects and through narrow-pore tubes. The force to do this comes from surface tension.

carbohydrate: a compound containing only carbon, hydrogen and oxygen. Carbohydrates have the formula $C_n(H_2O)_n$, where n is variable. *Example:* glucose ($C_6H_{12}O_6$).

carbonate: a salt of carbonic acid. Carbonate ions have the chemical formula CO_3^{2-}. *Examples:* calcium nitrate $CaCO_3$ and sodium carbonate Na_2CO_3.

catalyst: a substance that speeds up a chemical reaction but itself remains unaltered at the end of the reaction. *Example:* copper in the reaction of hydrochloric acid with zinc.

catalytic converter: a device incorporated into some exhaust systems. The catalytic converter contains a framework or granules with a very large surface area and coated with catalysts that convert the pollutant gases passing over them into harmless products.

cathode: the electrode at which reduction occurs; the positive terminal of a battery or the negative electrode of an electrolysis cell.

cathodic protection: the technique of protecting a metal object by connecting it to a more readily oxidizable metal. The metal object being protected is made into the cathode of a cell. *Example:* iron can be protected by coupling it with magnesium. Iron forms the cathode and magnesium the anode.

cation: a positively charged ion. *Examples:* calcium ion (Ca^{2+}), ammonium ion (NH_4^+).

caustic: a substance that can cause burns if it touches the skin. *Example:* Sodium hydroxide, caustic soda (NaOH).

Celsius scale (°C): a temperature scale on which the freezing point of water is at 0 degrees, and the normal boiling point at standard atmospheric pressure is 100 degrees.

cell: a vessel containing two electrodes and an electrolyte that can act as an electrical conductor.

centrifuge: an instrument for spinning small samples very rapidly. The fast spin makes the components of a mixture that have a different density separate, as in filtration.

ceramic: a material based on clay minerals that has been heated so that it has chemically hardened.

chalcogens: the members of Group 6 of the Periodic Table: oxygen, sulfur, selenium and tellurium. The word comes from the Greek meaning "brass giver," because all these elements are found in copper ores, and copper is the most important metal in making brass.

change of state: a change between two of the three states of matter, solid, liquid, and gas. *Example:* when water evaporates it changes from a liquid to a gaseous state.

Charles's Law: The volume (V) of a given mass of gas at constant pressure is directly proportional to its absolute temperature (T): $V \propto T$.

chromatography: A separation technique uses the ability of surfaces to adsorb substances with different strengths. The substances with the least adherence to the surface move faster and leave behind those that adhere more strongly.

coagulation: a term describing the tendency of small particles to stick together in clumps.

coherent: meaning that a substance holds together or sticks together well, and without holes or other defects. *Example:* Aluminum appears unreactive because, as soon as new metal is exposed to air, it forms a very complete oxide coating, which then stops further reaction occurring.

coinage metals: the elements copper, silver, and gold, used to make coins.

coke: a solid substance left after the gases have been extracted from coal.

colloid: a mixture of ultramicroscopic particles dispersed uniformly through a second substance to form a suspension that may be almost like a solution or may set to a jelly (gel). The word comes from the Greek for glue.

colorimeter: an instrument for measuring the light-absorbing power of a substance. The absorption gives an accurate indication of the concentration of some colored solutions.

combustion: a reaction in which an element or compound is oxidized to release energy. Some combustion reactions are slow, such as the combustion of the sugar we eat to provide energy. If the combustion results in a flame, it is called burning. A flame occurs where *gases* combust and release heat and light. At least two gases are therefore required if there is to be a flame. *Example:* the combustion or burning of methane gas (CH_4) in oxygen gas (O_2) produces carbon dioxide (CO_2)

and water (H_2O) and gives out heat and light. Some combustion reactions produce light and heat but do not produce flames. *Example:* the combustion of carbon in oxygen produces an intense red-white light but no flame.

combustion spoon: also known as a deflagrating spoon, it consists of a long metal handle with a small cup at the end. Its purpose is to allow the safe introduction of a (usually heated) substance into a filled gas jar, when the reaction is likely to be vigorous. *Example:* the introduction of a heated sodium pellet into a gas jar containing chlorine.

compound: a chemical consisting of two or more elements chemically bonded together. *Example:* Calcium atoms can combine with carbon atoms and oxygen atoms to make calcium carbonate ($CaCO_3$), a compound of all three atoms.

condensation: the formation of a liquid from a gas. This is a change of state, also called a phase change.

condensation nuclei: microscopic particles of dust, salt, and other materials suspended in the air that attract water molecules. The usual result is the formation of water droplets.

condensation polymer: a polymer formed by a chain of reactions in which a water molecule is eliminated as every link of the polymer is formed. *Examples:* polyesters, proteins, nylon.

conduction: (i) the exchange of heat (heat conduction) by contact with another object, or (ii) allowing the flow of electrons (electrical conduction).

conductivity: the ability of a substance to conduct. The conductivity of a solution depends on there being suitable free ions in the solution. A conducting solution is called an electrolyte. *Example:* dilute sulfuric acid.

convection: the exchange of heat energy with the surroundings produced by the flow of a fluid due to being heated or cooled.

corrosion: the oxidation of a metal. Corrosion is often regarded as unwanted and is more generally used to refer to the *slow* decay of a metal resulting from contact with gases and liquids in the environment. *Example:* Rust is the corrosion of iron.

corrosive: causing corrosion. *Example:* Sodium hydroxide (NaOH).

covalent bond: this is the most common form of strong chemical bonding and occurs when two atoms *share* electrons. *Example:* oxygen (O_2)

cracking: breaking down complex molecules into simpler compounds, as in oil refining.

crucible: a small bowl with a lip, made of heat-resistant white glazed ceramic. It is used for heating substances using a Bunsen flame.

crude oil: a chemical mixture of petroleum liquids. Crude oil forms the raw material for an oil refinery.

crystal: a substance that has grown freely so that it can develop external faces. Compare with crystalline, where the atoms are not free to form individual crystals, and amorphous, where the atoms are arranged irregularly.

crystalline: a solid in which the atoms, ions, or molecules are organized into an orderly pattern without distinct crystal faces. *Examples:* copper(II) sulfate, sodium chloride. Compare amorphous.

crystallization: the process in which a solute comes out of solution slowly and forms crystals. *See:* water of crystallization.

crystal systems: seven patterns or systems into which all crystals can be grouped: cubic, hexagonal, rhombohedral, tetragonal, orthorhombic, monoclinic, and triclinic.

cubic crystal system: groupings of crystals that look like cubes.

current: an electric current is produced by a flow of electrons through a conducting solid or ions through a conducting liquid. The rate of supply of this charge is measured in amperes (A).

decay (radioactive decay): the way that a radioactive element changes into another element due to loss of mass through radiation. *Example:* uranium 238 decays with the loss of an alpha particle to form thorium 234.

decomposition: the break down of a substance (for example, by heat or with the aid of a catalyst) into simpler components. In such a chemical reaction only one substance is involved. *Example:* hydrogen peroxide ($H_2O_2(aq)$) into oxygen ($O_2(g)$) and water ($H_2O(l)$).

decrepitation: when, as part of the decomposition of a substance, cracking sounds are also produced. *Example:* heating of lead nitrate ($Pb(NO_3)_2$).

dehydration: the removal of water from a substance by heating it, placing it in a dry atmosphere, or using a drying (dehydrating) reagent such as concentrated sulfuric acid.

density: the mass per unit volume (e.g., g/cc).

desalinization: the removal of all the salts from sea water, by reverse osmosis or heating the water and collecting the distillate. It is a very energy-intensive process.

desiccant: a substance that absorbs water vapor from the air. *Example:* silica gel.

desiccator: a lidded glass bowl containing a shelf. The apparatus is designed to store materials in dry air. A desiccant is placed below the shelf, and the substance to be dried is placed on the shelf. The lid makes a gas-tight joint with the bowl.

destructive distillation: the heating of a material so that it decomposes entirely to release all of its volatile components. Destructive distillation is also known as pyrolysis.

detergent: a chemical based on petroleum that removes dirt.

Devarda's alloy: zinc with a trace of copper that acts as a catalyst for reactions with the zinc.

diaphragm: a semipermeable membrane – a kind of ultrafine mesh filter – that allows only small ions to pass through. It is used in the electrolysis of brine.

diffusion: the slow mixing of one substance with another until the two substances are evenly mixed. Mixing occurs because of differences in concentration within the mixture. Diffusion works rapidly with gases, very slowly with liquids.

diffusion combustion: the form of combustion that occurs when two gases just begin to mix during ignition. As a result, the flame is hollow and yellow in color. *Example:* a candle flame.

dilute acid: an acid whose concentration has been reduced in a large proportion of water.

disinfectant: a chemical that kills bacteria and other microorganisms.

displacement reaction: a reaction that occurs because metals differ in their reactivity. If a more reactive metal is placed in a solution of a less reactive metal compound, a reaction occurs in which the more reactive metal displaces the metal ions in the solution. *Example:* when zinc metal is introduced into a solution of copper(II) sulfate (which thus contains copper ions), zinc goes into solution as zinc ions, while copper is displaced from the solution and forced to precipitate as metallic copper.

dissociate: to break bonds apart. In the case of acids it means to break up forming hydrogen ions. This is an example of ionization. Strong acids dissociate completely. Weak acids are not completely ionized, and a solution of a weak acid has a relatively low concentration of hydrogen ions.

dissolve: to break down a substance in a solution without causing a reaction.

distillation: the process of separating mixtures by condensing the vapors through cooling.

distilled water: distilled water is nearly pure water and is produced by distillation of tap water. Distilled water is used in the laboratory in preference to tap water because the distillation process removes many of the impurities in tap water that may influence the chemical reactions for which the water is used.

Dreschel bottle: a tall bottle with a special stopper designed to allow a gas to pass through a liquid. The stopper contains both inlet and outlet tubes. One tube extends below the surface of the liquid so that the gas has to pass through the liquid before it can escape to the outlet tube.

dropper funnel: a special funnel with a tap to allow the controlled release of a liquid. Also known as a dropping funnel or tap funnel.

drying agent: *See:* dehydrating agent.

dye: a colored substance that will stick to another substance so that both appear colored.

effervesce: to give off bubbles of gas.

effloresce: to lose water and turn to a fine powder on exposure to the air. *Example:* Sodium carbonate on the rim of a reagent bottle stopper.

electrical conductivity: *See:* conductivity

electrical potential: the energy produced by an electrochemical cell and measured by the voltage or electromotive force (emf). *See:* potential difference, electromotive force.

electrochemical cell: a cell consisting of two electrodes and an electrolyte. It can be set up to generate an electric current (usually known as a galvanic cell, an example of which is a battery), or an electric current can be passed through it to produce a chemical reaction (in which case it is called an electrolytic cell and can be used to refine metals or for electroplating).

electrochemical series: the arrangement of substances that are either oxidizing or reducing agents in order of strength as a reagent, for example, with the strong oxidizing agents at the top of the list and the strong reducing agents at the bottom.

electrode: a conductor that forms one terminal of a cell.

electrolysis: an electrical-chemical process that uses an electric current to cause the breakup of a compound and the movement of metal ions in a solution. The process happens in many natural situations (as for example in rusting) and is also commonly used in industry for purifying (refining) metals or for plating metal objects with a fine, even metal coating.

electrolyte: an ionic solution that conducts electricity.

electrolytic cell: *See:* electrochemical cell

electromotive force (emf): the force set up in an electric circuit by a potential difference.

electron: a tiny, negatively charged particle that is part of an atom. The flow of electrons through a solid material such as a wire produces an electric current.

electron configuration: the pattern in which electrons are arranged in shells around the nucleus of an atom. *Example:* chlorine has the configuration 2, 8, 7.

electroplating: depositing a thin layer of a metal onto the surface of another substance using electrolysis.

element: a substance that cannot be decomposed into simpler substance by chemical means. *Examples:* calcium, iron, gold.

emulsion: tiny droplets of one substance dispersed in another. One common oil in water emulsion is called milk. Because the tiny droplets tend to come together, another stabilizing substance is often needed. Soaps and detergents are such agents, wrapping the particles of grease and oil in a stable coat. Photographic film is an example of a solid emulsion.

endothermic reaction: a reaction that takes in heat. *Example:* when ammonium chloride is dissolved in water.

end point: the stage in a titration when the reaction between the titrant (added from a burette) and the titrate (in the flask) is complete. The end point is normally recognized by use of an indicator that has been added to the titrate. In an acid-base reaction this is also called the neutralization point.

enzyme: biological catalysts in the form of proteins in the body that speed up chemical reactions. Every living cell contains hundreds of enzymes that help the processes of life continue.

ester: organic compounds formed by the reaction of an alcohol with an acid and which often have a fruity taste. *Example:* ethyl acetate $(CH_3COOC_2H_5)$.

evaporation: the change of state of a liquid to a gas. Evaporation happens below the boiling point and is used as a method of separating the materials in a solution.

excess, to: if a reactant has been added to another reactant in excess, it has exceeded the amount required to complete the reaction.

exothermic reaction: a reaction that gives out substantial amounts of heat. *Example:* sucrose and concentrated sulfuric acid.

explosive: a substance that, when a shock is applied to it, decomposes very rapidly, releasing a very large amount of heat and creating a large volume of gases as a shock wave.

fat: semisolid, energy-rich compounds derived from plants or animals, made of carbon, hydrogen, and oxygen.

ferment: to break down a substance by microorganisms in the absence of oxygen. *Example:* fermentation of sugar to ethyl alcohol during the production of alcoholic drinks.

filtrate: the liquid that has passed through a filter.

filtration: the separation of a liquid from a solid using a membrane with small holes (i.e. a filter paper).

flame: a mixture of gases undergoing burning. A solid or liquid must produce a gas before it can react with oxygen and burn with a flame.

flammable (also inflammable): able to burn (in air). *Opposite:* nonflammable.

flocculation: the grouping together of small particles in a suspension to form particles large enough to settle out as a precipitate. Flocculation is usually caused by the presence of a flocculating agent. *Example:* calcium ions are the flocculating agent for suspended clay particles.

fluid: able to flow; either a liquid or a gas.

fluorescent: a substance that gives out visible light when struck by invisible waves, such as ultraviolet rays.

flux: a material used to make it easier for a liquid to flow. A flux dissolves metal oxides and so prevents a metal from oxidizing while being heated.

foam: a substance that is sufficiently gelatinous to be able to contain bubbles of gas. The gas bulks up the substance, making it behave as though it were semirigid.

fossil fuels: hydrocarbon compounds that have been formed from buried plant and animal remains. High pressures and temperatures lasting over millions of years are required. *Examples*: The fossil fuels are coal, oil and natural gas.

fraction: a group of similar components of a mixture. *Example:* In the petroleum industry the light fractions of crude oil are those with the smallest molecules, while the medium and heavy fractions have larger molecules.

fractional distillation: the separation of the components of a liquid mixture by heating them to their boiling points.

fractionating column: a glass column designed to allow different fractions to be separated when they boil. In industry it may be called a fractionating tower.

free radical: a very reactive atom or group with a "spare" electron. *Example:* methyl, $CH_3\bullet$.

freezing point: the temperature at which a substance undergoes a phase change from a liquid to a solid. It is the same temperature as the melting point.

fuel: a concentrated form of chemical energy. The main sources of fuels (called fossil fuels because they were formed by geological processes) are coal, crude oil, and natural gas.

fuel rods: the rods of uranium or other radioactive material used as a fuel in nuclear power plants.

fume chamber or fume cupboard: a special laboratory chamber fitted with a protective glass shield and containing a powerful extraction fan to remove toxic fumes.

fuming: an unstable liquid that gives off a gas. Very concentrated acid solutions are often fuming solutions. *Example:* fuming nitric acid.

galvanizing: applying a thin zinc coating to protect another metal.

gamma rays: waves of radiation produced as the nucleus of a radioactive element rearranges itself into a tighter cluster of protons and neutrons. Gamma rays carry enough energy to damage living cells.

gangue: the unwanted material in an ore.

gas/gaseous phase: a form of matter in which the molecules form no definite shape and are free to move about to uniformly fill any vessel they are put in. A gas can easily be compressed into a much smaller volume.

gas syringe: a glass syringe with a graduated cylinder designed to collect and measure small amounts of gases produced during an experiment.

gelatinous precipitate: a precipitate that has a jelly-like appearance. *Example:* iron (III) hydroxide. Because a gelatinous precipitate is mostly water, it is of a similar density to water and will float or lie suspended in the liquid. *See:* granular precipitate.

glass: a transparent silicate without any crystal growth. It has a glassy luster and breaks with a curved fracture. Note that some minerals have all these features and are therefore natural glasses. Household glass is a synthetic silicate.

glucose: the most common of the natural sugars ($C_6H_{12}O_6$). It occurs as the polymer known as cellulose, the fiber in plants. Starch is also a form of glucose.

granular precipitate: a precipitate that has a grainlike appearance. *Example:* lead(II) hydroxide. *See:* gelatinous precipitate.

gravimetric analysis: a quantitative form of analysis in which the mass (weight) of the reactants and products is measured.

group: a vertical column in the Periodic Table. There are eight groups in the table. Their numbers correspond to the number of electrons in the outer shell of the atoms in the group. *Example:* Group 1: member, sodium.

Greenhouse Effect: an increase in the global air temperature as a result of heat released from burning fossil fuels being absorbed by carbon dioxide in the atmosphere.

Greenhouse gas: any of various gases that contribute to the Greenhouse Effect. *Example:* carbon dioxide.

half-life: the time it takes for the radiation coming from a sample of a radioactive element to decrease by half.

halide: a salt of one of the halogens.

halogen: one of a group of elements including chlorine, bromine, iodine, and fluorine in Group 7 of the Periodic Table.

heat: the energy that is transferred when a substance is at a different temperature than its surroundings. *See:* endothermic and exothermic reactions.

heat capacity: the ratio of the heat supplied to a substance compared to the rise in temperature that is produced.

heat of combustion: the amount of heat given off by a mole of a substance during combustion. This heat is a property of the substance and is the same no matter what kind of combustion is involved. *Example:* heat of combustion of carbon is 94.05 kcal (✗ 4.18 = 393.1 kJ).

hydrate: a solid compound in crystalline form that contains water molecules. Hydrates commonly form when a solution of a soluble salt is evaporated. The water that forms part of a hydrate crystal is known as the "water of crystallization." It can usually be removed by heating, leaving an anhydrous salt.

hydration: the process of absorption of water by a substance. In some cases hydration makes the substance change color; in many other cases there is no color change, simply a change in volume. *Example:* dark blue hydrated copper(II) sulfate ($CuSO_4•5H_2O$) can be heated to produce white anhydrous copper(II) sulfate ($CuSO_4$).

hydride: a compound containing just hydrogen and another element, most often a metal. *Examples:* water (H_2O), methane (CH_4) and phosphine (PH_3).

hydrous: hydrated with water. *See:* anhydrous.

hydrocarbon: a compound in which only hydrogen and carbon atoms are present. Most fuels are hydrocarbons, as is the simple plastic polyethylene. *Example:* methane CH_4.

hydrogen bond: a type of attractive force that holds one molecule to another. It is one of the weaker forms of intermolecular attractive force. *Example:* hydrogen bonds occur in water.

ignition temperature: the temperature at which a substance begins to burn.

immiscible: will not mix with another substance. e.g., oil and water.

incandescent: glowing or shining with heat. *Example:* tungsten filament in an incandescent light bulb.

incomplete combustion: combustion in which only some of the reactant or reactants combust, or the products are not those that would be obtained if all the reactions went to completion. It is uncommon for combustion to be complete, and incomplete combustion is more frequent. *Example:* incomplete combustion of carbon in oxygen produces carbon monoxide and not carbon dioxide.

indicator (acid-base indicator): a substance or mixture of substances used to test the acidity or alkalinity of a substance. An indicator changes color depending on the acidity of the solution being tested. Many indicators are complicated organic substances. Some indicators used in the laboratory include Universal Indicator, litmus, phenolphthalein, methyl orange and bromothymol. *See:* Universal Indicator.

induction period: the time taken for a reaction to reach ignition temperature. During this period no apparent reaction occurs; then the materials appear to undergo spontaneous combustion.

inert: unreactive.

inhibitor: a substance that prevents a reaction from occurring.

inorganic substance: a substance that does not contain carbon and hydrogen. Examples: NaCl, $CaCO_3$.

insoluble: a substance that will not dissolve.

ion: an atom, or group of atoms, that has gained or lost one or more

electrons and so developed an electrical charge. Ions behave differently than electrically neutral atoms and molecules. They can move in an electric field, and they can also bind strongly to solvent molecules such as water. Positively charged ions are called cations; negatively charged ions are called anions. Ions can carry an electrical current through solutions.

ionic bond: the form of bonding that occurs between two ions when the ions have opposite charges. *Example:* sodium cations bond with chloride anions to form common salt (NaCl) when a salty solution is evaporated. Ionic bonds are strong bonds except in the presence of a solvent. *See:* bond.

ionic compound: a compound that consists of ions. *Example:* NaCl.

ionize: to break up neutral molecules into oppositely charged ions or to convert atoms into ions by the loss of electrons.

ionization: a process that creates ions.

isotope: an atom that has the same number of protons in its nucleus, but which has a different mass. *Example:* carbon 12 and carbon 14.

Kipp's apparatus: a piece of glassware consisting of three chambers, designed to provide a continuous and regulated production of gas by bringing the reactants into contact in a controlled way.

lanthanide series or lanthanide metals: a series of 15 similar metallic elements between lanthanum and lutetium. They are transition metals and are also called rare earths.

latent heat: the amount of heat that is absorbed or released during the process of changing state between gas, liquid, or solid. For example, heat is absorbed when a substance melts, and it is released again when the substance solidifies.

lattice: a regular arrangement of atoms, ions, or molecules in a crystalline solid.

leaching: the extraction of a substance by percolating a solvent through a material. *Example:* when water flows through an ore, some of the heavy metals in it may be leached out causing environmental pollution.

Liebig condenser: a piece of glassware consisting of a sloping, water-cooled tube. The design allows a volatile material to be condensed and collected.

liquefaction: to make something liquid.

liquid/liquid phase: a form of matter that has a fixed volume but no fixed shape.

lime (quicklime): calcium oxide (CaO). A white, caustic solid manufactured by heating limestone and used for making mortar, fertilizer, or bleach.

limewater: an aqueous solution of calcium hydroxide used especially to detect the presence of carbon dioxide.

litmus: an indicator obtained from lichens. Used as a solution or impregnated into paper (litmus paper) that is dampened before use. Litmus turns red under acid conditions and purple in alkaline conditions. Litmus is a crude indicator when compared with Universal Indicator.

load (electronics): an impedance or circuit that receives or develops the output of a cell or other power supply.

luster: the shininess of a substance.

malleable: able to be pressed or hammered into shape.

manometer: a device for measuring gas pressure. A simple manometer is made by partly filling a U-shaped rubber tube with water and connecting one end to the source of gas whose pressure is to be measured. The pressure is always relative to atmospheric pressure.

mass: the amount of matter in an object. In everyday use the word weight is often used (somewhat incorrectly) to mean mass.

matter: anything that has mass and takes up space.

melting point: the temperature at which a substance changes state from a solid phase to a liquid phase. It is the same as freezing point.

membrane: a thin flexible sheet. A semipermeable membrane has microscopic holes of a size that will selectively allow some ions and molecules to pass through but hold others back. It thus acts as a kind of filter. *Example:* a membrane used for osmosis.

meniscus: the curved surface of a liquid that forms in a small-bore or capillary tube. The meniscus is convex (bulges upward) for mercury and is concave (sags downward) for water.

metal: a class of elements that is a good conductor of electricity and heat, has a metallic luster, is malleable and ductile, forms cations, and has oxides that are bases. Metals are formed as cations held together by a sea of electrons. A metal may also be an alloy of these elements. *Example:* sodium, calcium, gold. *See:* alloy, metalloid, nonmetal.

metallic bonding: cations reside in a "sea" of mobile electrons. It allows metals to be good conductors and means that they are not brittle. *See:* bonding.

metallic luster: *See:* luster.

metalloid: a class of elements intermediate in properties between metals and nonmetals. Metalloids are also called semimetals or semiconductors. *Example:* silicon, germanium, antimony. *See:* metal, nonmetal, semiconductor.

micronutrient: an element that the body requires in small amounts. Another term is trace element.

mineral: a solid substance made of just one element or compound. *Example:* calcite is a mineral because it consists only of calcium carbonate; halite is a mineral because it contains only sodium chloride.

mineral acid: an acid that does not contain carbon and which attacks minerals. Hydrochloric, sulfuric, and nitric acids are the main mineral acids.

miscible: capable of being mixed.

mixing combustion: the form of combustion that occurs when two gases thoroughly mix before they ignite and so produce almost complete combustion. *Example:* when a Bunsen flame is blue.

mixture: a material that can be separated into two or more substances using physical means. *Example:* a mixture of copper(II) sulfate and cadmium sulfide can be separated by filtration.

molar mass: the mass per mole of atoms of an element. It has the same value and uses the same units as atomic weight. *Example:* molar mass of chlorine is 35.45 g/mol. *See:* atomic weight.

mole: 1 mole is the amount of a substance that contains Avagadro's number (6×10^{23}) of particles. *Example:* 1 mole of carbon-12 weighs exactly 12 g.

molecular mass: *See:* molar mass.

molecular weight: *See:* molar mass.

molecule: a group of two or more atoms held together by chemical bonds. *Example:* O_2.

monoclinic system: a grouping of crystals that look like double-ended chisel blades.

monomer: a small molecule and building block for larger chain molecules or polymers ("mono"

means one, "mer" means part). *Examples*: tetrafluoroethene for teflon, ethene for polyethene.

native element: an element that occurs in an uncombined state. *Examples*: sulfur, gold.

native metal: a pure form of a metal, not combined as a compound. Native metal is more common in poorly reactive elements than in those that are very reactive. *Examples*: copper, gold.

net ionic reaction: the overall, or net, change that occurs in a reaction, seen in terms of ions.

neutralization: the reaction of acids and bases to produce a salt and water. The reaction causes hydrogen from the acid and hydroxide from the base to be changed to water. *Example:* hydrochloric acid reacts with, and neutralizes, sodium hydroxide to form the salt sodium chloride (common salt) and water. The term is more generally used for any reaction in which the pH changes toward 7.0, which is the pH of a neutral solution. *See:* pH.

neutralization point: *See:* end point.

neutron: a particle inside the nucleus of an atom that is neutral and has no charge.

newton (N): the unit of force required to give one kilogram an acceleration of one meter per second every second (1 ms^{-2}).

nitrate: a compound that includes nitrogen and oxygen and contains more oxygen than a nitrite. Nitrate ions have the chemical formula NO_3^-. *Examples:* sodium nitrate $NaNO_3$ and lead nitrate $Pb(NO_3)_2$.

nitrite: a compound that includes nitrogen and oxygen and contains less oxygen than a nitrate. Nitrite ions have the chemical formula NO_2^-. *Example:* sodium nitrite $NaNO_2$.

noble gases: the members of Group 8 of the Periodic Table: helium, neon, argon, krypton, xenon, radon. These gases are almost entirely unreactive.

noble metals: silver, gold, platinum, and mercury. These are the least reactive metals.

noncombustible: a substance that will not combust or burn. *Example:* carbon dioxide.

nonmetal: a brittle substance that does not conduct electricity. *Examples:* sulfur, phosphorus, all gases. *See:* metal, metalloid.

normal salt: salts that do not contain a hydroxide (OH^-) ion, which would make them basic salts, or a hydrogen ion, which would make them acid salts. *Example:* sodium chloride ($NaCl$).

nucleus: the small, positively charged particle at the center of an atom. The nucleus is responsible for most of the mass of an atom.

opaque: a substance that will not transmit light so that it is impossible to see through it. Most solids are opaque.

ore: a rock containing enough of a useful substance to make mining it worthwhile. *Example:* bauxite, aluminum ore.

organic acid: an acid containing carbon and hydrogen. *Example:* methanoic (formic) acid ($HCOOH$).

organic chemistry: the study of organic compounds.

organic compound (organic substance; organic material): a compound (or substance) that contains carbon and usually hydrogen. (The carbonates are usually excluded.) *Examples:* methane (CH_4), chloromethane (CH_3Cl), ethene (C_2H_4), ethanol (C_2H_5OH), ethanoic acid (C_2H_3OOH) etc.

organic solvent: an organic substance that will dissolve other substances. *Example:* carbon tetrachloride (CCl_4).

osmosis: a process whereby molecules of a liquid solvent move through a semipermeable membrane from a region of low concentration of a solute to a region with a high concentration of a solute.

oxidation-reduction reaction (redox reaction): reaction in which oxidation and reduction occurs; a reaction in which electrons are transferred. *Example:* copper and oxygen react to produce copper(II) oxide. The copper is oxidized, and oxygen is reduced.

oxidation: combination with oxygen or a reaction in which an atom, ion, or molecule loses electrons to an oxidizing agent. (Note that an oxidizing agent does not have to contain oxygen.) The opposite of oxidation is reduction. *See:* reduction.

oxidation number (oxidation state): the effective charge on an atom in a compound. An increase in oxidation number corresponds to oxidation, and a decrease to reduction. Shown in Roman numerals. *Example:* manganate(IV).

oxidation state: *See:* oxidation number.

oxide: a compound that includes oxygen and one other element. *Example:* copper oxide (CuO).

oxidize: to combine with or gain oxygen or to react such that an atom, ion, or molecule loses electrons to an oxidizing agent.

oxidizing agent: a substance that removes electrons from another substance being oxidized (and therefore is itself reduced) in a redox reaction. *Example:* chlorine (Cl_2).

ozone: a form of oxygen whose molecules contain three atoms of oxygen. Ozone is regarded as a beneficial gas when high in the atmosphere because it blocks ultraviolet rays. It is a harmful gas when breathed in, so low-level ozone that is produced as part of city smog is regarded as a form of pollution. The ozone layer is the uppermost part of the stratosphere.

partial pressure: the pressure a gas in a mixture would exert if it alone occupied a flask. *Example:* oxygen makes up about a fifth of the atmosphere. Its partial pressure is therefore about a fifth of normal atmospheric pressure.

pascal: the unit of pressure, equal to one newton per square meter of surface. *See:* newton.

patina: a surface coating that develops on metals and protects them from further corrosion. *Example:* the green coating on copper carbonate that forms on copper statues.

percolate: to move slowly through the pores of a rock.

period: a row in the Periodic Table.

Periodic Table: a chart organizing elements by atomic number and chemical properties into groups and periods.

pestle and mortar: a pestle is a ceramic rod with a rounded end; a mortar is a ceramic dish. Pestle and mortar are used together to pound or grind solids into fine powders.

Petri dish: a shallow glass or plastic dish with a lid.

petroleum: a natural mixture of a range of gases, liquids, and solids derived from the decomposed remains of plants and animals.

pH: a measure of the hydrogen ion concentration in a liquid. Neutral is pH 7.0; numbers greater than this are alkaline; smaller numbers are acidic. *See:* neutralization, acid, base.

pH meter: a device that accurately measures the pH of a solution. A

pH meter is a voltmeter that measures the electric potential difference between two electrodes (which are attached to the meter through a probe) when they are submerged in a solution. The readings are shown on a dial or digital display.

phase: a particular state of matter. A substance may exist as a solid, liquid, or gas and may change between these phases with addition or removal of energy. *Examples:* ice, liquid, and vapor are the three phases of water. Ice undergoes a phase change to water when heat energy is added.

phosphor: any material that glows when energized by ultraviolet or electron beams such as in fluorescent tubes and cathode ray tubes. Phosphors, such as phosphorus, emit light after the source of excitation is cut off. This is why they glow in the dark. By contrast, fluorescors, such as fluorite, only emit light while they are being excited by ultraviolet light or an electron beam.

photochemical smog: photochemical reactions are caused by the energy of sunlight. Photochemical smog is a mixture of tiny particles and a brown haze caused by the reaction of colorless nitric oxide from vehicle exhausts and oxygen of the air to form brown nitrogen dioxide.

photon: a parcel of light energy.

photosynthesis: the process by which plants use the energy of the Sun to make the compounds they need for life. In photosynthesis six molecules of carbon dioxide from the air combine with six molecules of water, forming one molecule of glucose (sugar) and releasing six molecules of oxygen back into the atmosphere.

pipe-clay triangle: a device made from three small pieces of ceramic tube that are wired together in the shape of a triangle. Pipe-clay

triangles are used to support round-bottomed dishes when they are heated in a Bunsen flame.

pipette: a log, slender glass tube used, in conjunction with a pipette filler, to draw up and then transfer accurately measured amounts of liquid.

plastic: (material) a carbon-based substance consisting of long chains (polymers) of simple molecules. The word plastic is commonly restricted to synthetic polymers. *Examples:* polyvinyl chloride, nylon: **(property)** a material is plastic if it can be made to change shape easily. Plastic materials will remain in the new shape. (Compare with elastic, a property whereby a material goes back to its original shape.)

pneumatic trough: a shallow water-filled glass dish used to house a beehive shelf and a gas jar as part of the apparatus for collecting a gas over water.

polar solvent: a solvent in which the atoms have partial electric charges. *Example:* water.

polymer: a compound that is made of long chains by combining molecules (called monomers) as repeating units. ("Poly" means many, "mer" means part.) *Examples:* polytetrafluoroethene or Teflon from tetrafluoroethene, Terylene from terephthalic acid and ethane-1,2-diol (ethylene glycol).

polymerization: a chemical reaction in which large numbers of similar molecules arrange themselves into large molecules, usually long chains. This process usually happens when there is a suitable catalyst present. *Example:* ethene gas reacts to form polyethene in the presence of certain catalysts.

polymorphism: (meaning many shapes) the tendency of some materials to have more than one solid form. *Example:* carbon as diamond, graphite and buckminsterfullerene.

porous: a material containing many small holes or cracks. Quite often the pores are connected, and liquids, such as water or oil, can move through them.

potential difference: a measure of the work that must be done to move an electric charge from one point to the other in a circuit. Potential difference is measured in volts, V. *See:* electrical potential.

precious metal: silver, gold, platinum, iridium and palladium. Each is prized for its rarity.

precipitate: a solid substance formed as a result of a chemical reaction between two liquids or gases. *Example:* iron (III) hydroxide is precipitated when sodium hydroxide solution is added to iron (III) chloride. *See:* gelatinous precipitate, granular precipitate.

preservative: a substance that prevents the natural organic decay processes from occurring. Many substances can be used safely for this purpose, including sulfites and nitrogen gas.

pressure: the force per unit area measured in pascals. *See:* pascal.

product: a substance produced by a chemical reaction. *Example:* when the reactants copper and oxygen react, they produce the product copper oxide.

proton: a positively charged particle in the nucleus of an atom that balances out the charge of the surrounding electrons.

proton number: this is the modern expression for atomic number. *See:* atomic number.

purify: to remove all impurities from a mixture, perhaps by precipitation or filtration.

pyrolysis: chemical decomposition brought about by heat. *Example:* decomposition of lead nitrate. *See:* destructive distillation.

pyrometallurgy: refining a metal from its ore using heat. A blast furnace or smelter is the main equipment used.

quantitative: measurement of the amounts of constituents of a substance, for example, by mass or volume. *See:* gravimetric analysis, volumetric analysis.

radiation: the exchange of energy with the surroundings through the transmission of waves or particles of energy. Radiation is a form of energy transfer that can happen through space; no intervening medium is required (as would be the case for conduction and convection).

radical: an atom, molecule, or ion with at least one unpaired electron. *Example:* nitrogen monoxide (NO).

radioactive: emitting radiation or particles from the nucleus of its atoms.

radioactive decay: a change in a radioactive element due to loss of mass through radiation. For example, uranium decays (changes) to lead.

reactant: a starting material that takes part in and undergoes change during a chemical reaction. *Example:* hydrochloric acid and calcium carbonate are reactants; the reaction produces the products calcium chloride, carbon dioxide, and water.

reaction: the recombination of two substances using parts of each substance to produce new substances. *Example:* the reactants sodium chloride and sulfuric acid react and recombine to form the products sodium sulfate, chlorine, and water.

reactivity: the tendency of a substance to react with other substances. The term is most widely used in comparing the reactivity of metals. Metals are arranged in a reactivity series.

reactivity series: the series of metals organized in order of their reactivity, with the most reactive metals, such as sodium, at the top and the least react metals, such as gold, at the bottom. Hydrogen is usually included in the series for comparative purposes.

reagent: a commonly available substance (reactant) used to create a reaction. Reagents are the chemicals normally kept on chemistry laboratory shelf. Many substances called reagents are most commonly used for test purposes.

redox reaction (oxidation-reduction reaction): a reaction that involves oxidation and reduction; a reactions in which electrons are transferred. *See:* oxidation-reduction.

reducing agent: a substance that gives electrons to another substance being reduced (and therefore itself being oxidized) in a redox reaction. *Example:* hydrogen sulfide (H_2S).

reduction: the removal of oxygen from, or the addition of hydrogen to, a compound. Also a reaction in which an atom, ion, or molecule gains electrons from a reducing agent. (The opposite of reduction is oxidation.)

reduction tube: a boiling tube with a small hole near the closed end. The tube is mounted horizontally, a sample is placed in the tube, and a reducing gas, such as carbon monoxide, is passed through the tube. The oxidized gas escapes through the small hole.

refining: separating a mixture into the simpler substances of which it is made.

reflux distillation system: a form of distillation using a Liebig condenser placed vertically, so that all the vapors created during boiling are condensed back into the liquid rather than escaping. In this way the concentration of all the reactants remains constant.

relative atomic mass: in the past a measure of the mass of an atom on a scale relative to the mass of an atom of hydrogen, where hydrogen is 1. Nowadays a measure of the mass of an atom relative to the mass of one twelfth of an atom of carbon-12. If the relative atomic mass is given as a rounded figure, it is called an approximate relative atomic mass. *Examples:* chlorine 35, calcium 40, gold 197. *See:* atomic mass, atomic weight.

reversible reaction: a reaction in which the products can be transformed back into their original chemical form. *Example:* heated iron reacts with steam to produce iron oxide and hydrogen. If the hydrogen is passed over this heated oxide it forms iron and steam. $3Fe + 4H_2O \rightleftharpoons Fe_3O_4 + 4H_2$.

roast: heating a substance for a long time at a high temperature, as in a furnace.

rust: the product of the corrosion of iron and steel in the presence of air and water.

salt: a compound, often involving a metal, that is the reaction product of an acid and a base, or of two elements. (Note "salt" is also the common word for sodium chloride, common salt, or table salt.) *Example:* sodium chloride ($NaCl$) and potassium sulfate (K_2SO_4) *See:* acid salt, basic salt, normal salt.

salt bridge: a permeable material soaked in a salt solution that allows ions to be transferred from one container to another. The salt solution remains unchanged during this transfer. *Example:* sodium sulfate used as a salt bridge in a galvanic cell.

saponification: a reaction between a fat and a base that produces a soap.

saturated: a state in which a liquid can hold no more of a substance. If any more of the substance is added, it will not dissolve.

saturated hydrocarbon: a hydrocarbon in which the carbon atoms are held with single bonds. *Example:* ethane (C_2H_4).

saturated solution: a solution that holds the maximum possible amount of dissolved material. When saturated, the rate of dissolving solid and that of recrystallization solid are the same, and a condition of equilibrium is reached. The amount of material in solution varies with the temperature; cold solutions can hold less dissolved solid material than hot solutions. Gases are more soluble in cold liquids than hot liquids.

sediment: material that settles out at the bottom of a liquid when it is still. A precipitate is one form of sediment.

semiconductor: a material of intermediate conductivity. Semiconductor devices often use silicon when they are made as part of diodes, transistors, or integrated circuits. Elements intermediate between metals and nonmetals are also sometimes called semiconductors. *Example:* germanium oxide, germanium. *See:* metalloid.

semipermeable membrane: a thin material that acts as a fine sieve or filter, allowing small molecules to pass, but holding large molecules back.

separating column: used in chromatography. A tall glass tube containing a porous disc near the base and filled with a substance (for example, aluminum oxide, which is known as a stationary phase) that can adsorb materials on its surface. When a mixture is passed through the column, fractions are retarded by differing amounts, so that each fraction is washed through the column in sequence.

separating funnel: a pear-shaped glassware funnel designed to permit the separation of immiscible liquids by simply pouring off the more dense liquid while leaving the less dense liquid in the funnel.

series circuit: an electrical circuit in which all of the components are joined end to end in a line.

shell: the term used to describe the imaginary ball-shaped surface outside the nucleus of an atom that would be formed by a set of electrons of similar energy. The outermost shell is known as the valence shell. *Example:* neon has shells containing 2 and 8 electrons.

side-arm boiling tube: a boiling tube with an integral glass pipe near its open end. The side arm is normally used for the entry or exit of a gas.

simple distillation: the distillation of a substance when only one volatile fraction is to be collected. Simple distillation uses a Liebig condenser arranged almost horizontally. When the liquid mixture is heated and vapors are produced, they enter the condenser and then flow away from the flask and can be collected. *Example:* simple distillation of ethanoic acid.

slag: a mixture of substances that are waste products of a furnace. Most slags are composed mainly of silicates.

smelting: roasting a substance in order to extract the metal contained in it.

smog: a mixture of smoke and fog. The term is used to describe city fogs in which there is a large proportion of particulate matter (tiny pieces of carbon from exhausts) and also a high concentration of sulfur and nitrogen gases and probably ozone. *See:* photochemical smog.

smokeless fuel: a fuel that has been subjected to partial pyrolysis so that there is no more loose particulate matter remaining. *Example:* Coke is a smokeless fuel.

solid/solid phase: a rigid form of matter that maintains its shape whatever its container.

solubility: the maximum amount of a substance that can be contained in a solvent.

soluble: readily dissolvable in a solvent.

solute: a substance that has dissolved. *Example:* sodium chloride in water.

solution: a mixture of a liquid (the solvent) and at least one other substance of lesser abundance (the solute). Mixtures can be separated by physical means, for example, by evaporation and cooling. *See:* aqueous solution.

solvent: the main substance in a solution.

spectator ions: the ionic part of a compound that does not play an active part in a reaction. *Example:* when magnesium ribbon is placed in copper(II) sulfate solution the copper is displaced from the solution by the magnesium while the sulfate ion (SO_4^{2-}) plays no part in the reaction and so behaves as a spectator ion.

spectrum: the range of colors that make up visible light (as seen in a rainbow) or across all electromagnetic radiation, arranged in progression according to their wavelength.

spontaneous combustion: the effect of a very reactive material or combination of reactants that suddenly reach their ignition temperature and begin to combust rapidly.

standard temperature and pressure (STP): 0°C at one atmosphere (a pressure that supports a column of mercury 760 mm high). Also given as 0°C at 100 kilopascals. *See:* atmospheric pressure.

state of matter: the physical form of matter. There are three states of matter: liquid, solid, and gaseous.

stationary phase: a name given to a material that is used as a medium for separating a liquid mixture, as in in chromatography.

strong acid: an acid that has completely dissociated (ionized) in water. Mineral acids are strong acids.

sublime/sublimation: the change of a substance from solid to gas, or vice versa, without going through a liquid phase. *Example:* iodine sublimes from a purple solid to a purple gas.

substance: a type of material, including mixtures.

sulfate: a compound that includes sulfur and oxygen and contains more oxygen than a sulfite. Sulfate ions have the chemical formula SO_4^{2-}. *Examples:* calcium sulfate $CaSO_4$ (the main constituent of gypsum) and aluminum sulfate $Al_2(SO_4)_3$ (an alum).

sulfide: a sulfur compound that contains no oxygen. Sulfide ions have the chemical formula S^{2-}. *Example:* hydrogen sulfide (H_2S).

sulfite: a compound that includes sulfur and oxygen but contains less oxygen than a sulfate. Sulfite ions have the chemical formula SO_3^{2-}. *Example:* sodium sulfite Na_2SO_3.

supercooling: the ability of some substances to cool below their normal freezing point. *Example:* sodium thiosulfate.

supersaturated solution: a solution in which the amount of solute is greater than what would normally be expected in a saturated solution. Most solids are more soluble in hot solutions than in cold. If a hot saturated solution is made up, the solution can be rapidly cooled down below its freezing point before it begins to solidify. This is a supersaturated solution.

surface tension: the force that operates on the surface of a liquid and that makes it act as though it were covered with an invisible, elastic film.

suspension: a mist of tiny particles in a liquid.

synthesis: a reaction in which a substance is formed from simpler reactants. *Example:* hydrogen gas and chlorine gas react to sythesize hydrogen chloride gas. The term can also be applied to polymerization of organic compounds.

synthetic: does not occur naturally but has to be manufactured. Commonly used in the name "synthetic fiber."

tare: an allowance made for the weight of a container.

tarnish: a coating that develops as a result of the reaction between a metal and substances in the air. The most common form of tarnishing is a very thin transparent oxide coating.

terminal: one of the electrodes of a battery.

test (chemical): a reagent or a procedure used to reveal the presence of another reagent. *Example:* litmus and other indicators are used to test the acidity or alkalinity of a substance.

test tube: A thin glass tube closed at one end and used for chemical tests, etc. The composition and thickness of the glass is such that while it is inert to most chemical reactions, it may not sustain very high temperatures but can usually be heated in a Bunsen flame. *See:* boiling tube.

thermal decomposition: the breakdown of a substance using heat: *See* pyrolysis.

thermoplastic: a plastic that will soften and can repeatedly be molded into shape on heating and

will set into the molded shape as it cools.

thermoset: a plastic that will set into a molded shape as it cools, but which cannot be made soft by reheating.

thistle funnel: a narrow tube, expanded at the top into a thistlehead-shaped vessel. It is used as a funnel when introducing small amounts of liquid reactant. When fitted with a tap, it can be used to control the rate of entry of a reactant. *See:* burette.

titration: the analysis of the composition of a substance in a solution by measuring the volume of that solution (the titrant, normally in a burette) needed to react with a given volume of another solution (the titrate, normally placed in a flask). An indicator is often used to signal change. *Example:* neutralization of sodium hydroxide using hydrochloric acid in an acid–base titration. *See:* end point.

toxic: poisonous.

transition metals: the group of metals that belong to the d-block of the Periodic Table. Transition metals commonly have a number of differently colored oxidation states. *Examples:* iron, vanadium.

Universal Indicator: a mixture of indicators commonly used in the laboratory because of its reliability. Used as a solution or impregnated into paper (Indicator paper) that is dampened before use. Universal Indicator changes color from purple in a strongly alkaline solution through green when the solution is neutral to red in strongly acidic solutions. Universal Indicator is more accurate than litmus paper but less accurate than a pH meter.

unsaturated hydrocarbon: a hydrocarbon in which at least one bond is a double or triple bond. Hydrogen atoms can be added to

unsaturated compounds to form saturated compounds. *Example:* ethene, C_2H_4 or $CH_2=CH_2$.

vacuum: a container from which air has been removed using a pump.

valency: the number of bonds that an atom can form. *Examples:* calcium has a valency of 2 and bromine a valency of 1

valency shell: the outermost shell of an atom. *See:* shell.

vapor: the gaseous phase of a substance. *See:* gas.

vein: a fissure in rock that has filled with ore or other mineral-bearing rock.

viscous: slow-moving, syrupy. A liquid that has a low viscosity is said to be mobile.

volatile: readily forms a gas.

volatile fraction: the part of a liquid mixture that will readily vaporize under the conditions prevailing during the reaction. *See:* fraction, vapor.

water of crystallization: the water molecules absorbed into the crystalline structure as a liquid changes to a solid. *Example:* hydrated copper(II) sulfate $CuSO_4•5H_2O$. *See:* hydrate.

weak acid and **weak base**: an acid or base that has only partly dissociated (ionized) in water. Most organic acids are weak acids. *See:* organic acid.

weight: the gravitational force on a substance. *See:* mass.

X-rays: a form of very short wave radiation.

MASTER INDEX